VAN DUSEN

The presence of other worlds

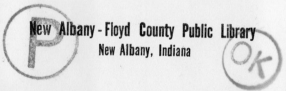

The Presence of Other Worlds

THE PRESENCE
OF OTHER WORLDS

The Psychological/Spiritual
Findings of Emanuel Swedenborg

WILSON VAN DUSEN

HARPER & ROW, PUBLISHERS
New York, Evanston, San Francisco, London

ACKNOWLEDGMENT

"Emanuel Swedenborg" is translated by Richard Howard and César Rennert. A selection from the book, JORGE LUIS BORGES: SELECTED POEMS 1923–1967, edited by Norman Thomas di Giovanni. English translations, copyright © 1968, 1970, 1971, 1972 by Emecé Editores, S. A., and Norman Thomas di Giovanni. A Seymour Lawrence Book/Delacorte Press. Used with permission of the publisher.

FIRST EDITION

Designed by Gloria Adelson

Library of Congress Cataloging in Publication Data

Van Dusen, Wilson, Miles.
    The presence of other worlds.
    Includes bibliographical references.
    1. Swedenborg, Emanuel, 1688–1772. I. Title.
BX8748.V3   230'.9'   73–18684
ISBN 0–06–068826–2

Dedicated to

Hugo Lj. Odhner, master scholar of

the most important of all subjects

Contents

Emanuel Swedenborg

Taller than the others, this man
Walked among them, at a distance,
Now and then calling the angels
By their secret names. He would see
That which earthly eyes do not see:
The fierce geometry, the crystal
Labyrinth of God and the sordid
Milling of infernal delights.
He knew that Glory and Hell too
Are in your soul, with all their myths;
He knew, like the Greek, that the days
Of time are Eternity's mirrors.
In dry Latin he went on listing
The unconditional Last Things.
                    —Jorge Luis Borges[1]

Introduction

Is it possible for a man to discover too much, so much that others will be puzzled by his works, put them aside, and suspect he is mad? Yes, it is possible, though perhaps very rare. This is an account of a man who journeyed too far and found too much.

Years ago a newspaper ad offered a free book that promised to clarify the whole of existence. I walked across town to get the book at a picturesque church from a kindly minister, Othmar Tobisch. The *Divine Providence* of Emanuel Swedenborg at first seemed rather abstract, dull, and a rehash of Christian ideas. It was slightly intriguing because the author was dealing with psychological and spiritual concepts simultaneously. I put aside the book. A few years later I went through a series of religious visions, which called me back to the book. It seemed to me that Swedenborg was talking about what I had experienced. This time I came to him with a more loving attentiveness. What had seemed dull and abstract now came alive as a man's description of his personal experiences in the worlds beyond this one. Swedenborg's description was much more detailed than my own experience, but it was apparent to me that we had similar experiences. In his quiet and somewhat ponderous way he was describing all the worlds beyond this one and relating them to this world.

Gradually I became accustomed to his style and vocabulary, for he was speaking to me across ▨▨ centuries of time. What impressed me most was that he was always speaking of actual experience. I was meeting the man Ralph Waldo Emerson included in his *Representative Men.* Emerson said, "A colossal soul (who) lies vast abroad on his times, uncomprehended by them, and requires ▨▨▨▨ focal distance to be seen. . . . One of the . . . mastodons of literature, he is not to be measured by whole colleges of ordinary scholars."²

As a clinical psychologist with religious leanings, it was a great pleasure to see a man moving easily in both realms like one life process. I started acquiring everything he ever wrote and everything I could find written about him. It took me ▨▨ years to get a photocopy of his *Journal of Dreams,* but it was impressive to see him struggling to understand his dreams and the internal guidance system they reflect. His five-volume *Spiritual Diary* was like a strange treasure trove of experiences with demons and spirits. Biographies on him clothed this man in human history. It was a relief to find a giant six-volume concordance of his works. For recreation it was possible to take an idea, such as insanity, and trace all he said on it through his many volumes. A few scholars helped clarify different areas with their distillations of his works. Gradually the vast, complex landscape of his writings became clear.

I had pursued all the principal writers in psychoanalysis and psychotherapy. Only Carl Jung even approached the stature of Swedenborg. Swedenborg knew personally, at first hand, that Self which Jung knew only by speculation on its symbolic manifestations. All other writers could be comprehended in short order. Swedenborg is so vast that I am pleased his books are available in heaven, so the matter can be pursued even there!

My purpose is simple, to bring Swedenborg within the reach of many. There are a number of keys to aid this grasp.

It is necessary to understand the age and circumstances in which he worked. He lived at the dawn of science in the eighteenth century. He himself mastered all the sciences of his day. Though the strange richness of his later psychological-spiritual findings would later get him labeled as either a great mystic or a madman, he never changed fundamentally from the scientist who simply wanted to understand and describe the whole of existence. When he finished all the known outer world, he started to work on the mind. He took an unusually direct and short route through the psyche. Many of his later religious followers are puzzled at his dreams, visions, trances, etc. Because the way he penetrated the psyche is so little known today, it is necessary to explain how he did it in some detail. This key, which makes a good deal of sense out of what he found, has largely been missing until now. If even the beginnings of his method are followed by average persons, they will make the same surprising discoveries that he made. Unfortunately, the whole inward journey he took is too dangerous and difficult for others to follow. Swedenborg was later to say that madness is possible along the path he took. There is little doubt of that. He released tremendous forces within his own mind. The inner guidance led him to personal discoveries and changes that at first did not seem entirely wise or safe. Only from the perspective of later years could he see the wisdom in the changes that had been wrought on him by this inner process. The changes in his personality and the growth in his approach to the Divine were to be essentially one process. Swedenborg was, in effect, feeling his way along in the dark recesses of the psyche toward the Divine. We have the advantage of two centuries of discoveries and modern psychology to clarify our understanding of what was occurring within him.

Swedenborg was looking for God within and was beginning to find This One. The price of his discovery was changes that would make him a much more humble and complete man. He had to meet and integrate much of his own unconscious. As he became a more appropriate instrument through these changes, the Hand of the Divine became more apparent. Finally, after scourging himself for a final and relatively persistent fault, he was introduced into heaven and hell. Perhaps many down through time had had glimpses of the worlds beyond this one, but Swedenborg was to have free and relatively constant access for many years. This claim alone becomes an obstacle to many to accept him. It sounds so immodest. Actually, this proud and great scientist became unusually modest before these other worlds were opened up to him. But it requires neither acceptance of Swedenborg's reliability nor one's own death to verify what he described. Because all the worlds beyond this one are imaged in the processes of mind, it is possible to check how accurately Swedenborg's description accords with our personal experience. It is no accident that the worlds beyond this are reflected in our mind. That is the way the mind was made. We are made in the image. We are the microscosm that reflects the macrocosm. Even if there were no heaven and hell, Swedenborg's description would remain a fascinating picture of all the mansions that make up mind and man's experience. Just as incidental details, there were a number of miracles associated with Swedenborg that suggest he had really entered other worlds. He didn't consider these important enough to even set down. Also, the strange visionary experiences of contemporary persons echo Swedenborg so closely as to suggest the current validity of his reports. ————

Visions and even heaven and hell are somewhat incidental to what Swedenborg was getting at. He says it is perfectly appropriate for mere man to ask and to seek to understand the whole of existence. The whole of existence, all the worlds, may be understood. But the root understanding, the fundament of all the rest, is how we relate to each other, what good we do or what use we serve. Here Swedenborg comes to the fundamental understanding of all religions. Though Swedenborg was very Christian, it is also clear that he was talking about the core of all religions. For after all, as he himself noted, all the religions are like different colored stones in the crown of The One King. In both his complexly simple psychology and his emphasis on how well we relate to each other, Swedenborg's whole journey to other worlds comes to earth in what everyone can understand and appreciate. Again, the vast and seemingly remote and the very near at hand turn out to be intimately related. The results of Swedenborg's journey in and understanding of all the worlds, when translated into the concrete realities of the present, provoke in most people a feeling of "Well, of course that's true." And truth is always of this character for him. It rests in the potentialities of the human (it is written on the heart) and can be recognized and experienced by everyone. Do you want to reach heaven? Are you now acting by the good you know? The far and the near, the psychological and the spiritual, the other worlds and this one can all be found in the now, and seem so matter-of-fact, so familiar when found.

I would like to thank the many followers of Swedenborg who have preserved, translated into over twenty languages, and published at cost his works for two centuries so that they might remain available. I wish to thank the Swedenborg Foundation of New York City for its generous support, with special thanks to Tomas Spiers and Virginia Branston. For a detailed review of the whole manuscript I thank Professor George Dole.

San Rafael, California
December 1973

1
The Man

Quite freely and boldly I stepped down a large stairway;
by and by there was a ladder, below it there was a hole
which went down to a great depth; it was difficult to get
to the other side without falling into the hole. On the other
side there were persons to whom I reached out my hand
to help them cross over, I awoke. It is the danger in which
I am of falling into the abyss, unless I receive help. JD 20*

So begins a most remarkable journey into inner space and the
worlds beyond. This is the privately recorded dream of
Emanuel Swedenborg, who may have been one of the most
gifted men to have ever lived. In itself the dream is remarkable enough. Though written over two centuries ago, the
dreamer reflects a modern understanding of the nature of
dreams. The dream is a dramatic representation of the present life of the dreamer. To get the most from it the dreamer
should identify with all parts of it. He could easily have
flattered himself as the helper of others. Yet he sees the

*See the Key to Abbreviations of Works Cited, p. 000.

danger as in him and he himself needs help.

But even more remarkable, this oldest and largest series of dreams and associations, written in 1744, was authored by a man who may have been among the last to have mastered all known knowledge. His attainments before he started work on his dreams were tremendous. He had exhausted all the known sciences after founding several of them. His discoveries about the human brain or his suggestion of the nebular hypothesis would have been sufficient for fame, recognition, and public acceptance. He could have quit at the age of fifty-six. Instead he took on psychology and religion.

His dreams were recorded at the time he was breaking into the inner realms; he discovered so much that his account became incredible. It was as though he found too much on this inner journey and described it too well in some thirty-six volumes. Future generations would not have time to digest all he found. In some respects he remained too far in advance of the findings of others for centuries. Critics would seize on one or more of his most unusual private journals and call him mad. But those who understood his discoveries would pray for a like madness. Most would come to think of him as an obscure mystic and overlook the fact that he had completed over one hundred works in all the known sciences. His later discoveries were so far-reaching and disturbing to our conventional views that they overshadowed all his earlier work. But before we follow the journey inward, it would be well to grasp who he was and how he lived. This firm base in his reality will make all the rest seem more probable.

VAPOR, FOG, MIST

The Life of Emanuel Swedenborg

The name "Emanuel" is biblical and means "God is with us." Swedenborg's father was a Lutheran bishop attached to the Swedish court. It is said that in another age his father would have been a saint. He believed in the presence of angels and demons and occasionally dealt with them, which was common for his time and place. He embarked on several publishing ventures, trying to enlighten his countrymen and improve public school education. For instance, he tried to make the Bible available to common men. He must have been too busy a church official to have been very close to his children.

Emanuel was the third of nine children. His mother died when he was only eight. For most of his formative years he lived in the university town of Uppsala. Relatively little is known of these years. He lived among conservative church and university people. Early feminine influences were his busy stepmother and his older sister Anna. He received a classical university education with a heavy emphasis on Latin, Greek, and literature to the level of a master's degree. His earliest published works were Latin poetry. The young Swedenborg was thought of as a poet.

From his early years Swedenborg had a tendency to speculate on ultimate questions. As a boy he long pondered religious issues and his father considered him a promising religious prodigy. The spirit of the father and son differed, though. The father simply accepted the reality of religion. The son examined, questioned, and speculated. At the time his father was elevated to the position of the archbishop of Skara, the young university student went to live with his brother-in-law Eric Benzelius, his senior by thirteen years. Benzelius was gifted with broad interests in science and Swedenborg found fertile ground for his need to search, question and find. The youthful Latin poet soon became a burgeoning scientist, somewhat to the dismay of his father.

Among his relatives and friends were some of Sweden's earliest scientists, including Christopher Polhem. Polhem promised his oldest daughter to Emanuel, but she married another man. Then he was promised the hand of a younger sister, Emerentia. She rejected Swedenborg, who released her from the formal contract. He swore then never to have any serious affairs with ladies, a promise he kept. There are many indications that he was highly attracted to women, and may have had mistresses in his early years, but he never married.

Swedenborg's family was moderately well off. His father was a professor of theology and a bishop and his stepmother had mining connections in her family. The young college graduate became a very practical man, searching out the best method of doing things or learning new sciences. It was as though all the energies a young man might devote to his family and job were devoted to learning. He lived on meager support from his father. Later his scientific works came to the attention of the king and he was appointed assessor of mines for Sweden. He was one of a handful of men who oversaw all aspects of Sweden's mining interests. This was the only actual job he ever held.

His penchant for knowledge was put to good use. He would travel in Europe, gather notes on the latest methods in mining, and introduce them in his own country. Thus many of his early inventions had to do with mining machinery. He toured Swedish mines on horseback, went down many a mine shaft, and suggested ways to improve methods. It appears he had considerable influence on Sweden's mining industry. In a way he was superior to the position, though it provided a salary when he needed it. Eventually he published a definitive, beautifully illustrated summary of all that was known of minerals.

Something of his hunger for science can be illustrated by the following excerpts from his letter to Eric Benzelius written when he was twenty-two.

With respect to the twenty-four foot telescope, I ordered the glasses for it at Marchal's who is said to be the only one patronized by the Royal Society. These glasses are beyond expectation expensive for they cost 40 shillings. . . .

I visit daily the best mathematicians here in town. I have been
with Flamsteed, who is considered the best astonomer in England,
and who is constantly taking observations, which, together with
Paris Observations, will give us some day a correct theory respecting the motion of the moon . . . and with its help there may be found
a true longitude at sea [a problem he would later solve]. HUBBLE SPACE
    Newton has laid a good foundation for correcting irregularities PILOT
of the moon in his *Principia;* he has however not yet published the
tables, but simply the theory; he has also corrected in it the preces-
sion of the equinoxes, and the periods of the tides.
    You encourage me to go on with my studies; but I think that I
ought rather to be discouraged, as I have such an *"immoderate
desire"* for them, especially for astronomy and mechanics. I also
turn my lodgings to some use, and change them often; at first I was
at a watchmaker's, and afterwards at a cabinet maker's, and now
I am at a mathematical instrument maker's, from them I steal their
trades, which some day will be of use to me. I have recently
computed for my own pleasure several useful tables for the latitude
of Upsal, and all the solar and lunar eclipses which will take place
between 1712 and 1721. Docs I, pp. 209 f.

When Swedenborg was thirty-one, the whole family was
ennobled. The name of Swedberg became Swedenborg,
thereby referring to the family estate. As the oldest son,
Baron Emanuel Swedenborg later took his position in the
Swedish House of Nobles. It is said that he never missed a
meeting even though he traveled all over Europe for years at
a time. Swedenborg was never comfortable speaking to
groups. He easily stammered when nervous, but he could
write. He wrote some of the more important bills, or
"memorials," on peace, the economy of the country, liquor
regulation, and other subjects.
    Being a leader of his country's mining and a nobleman
were only background, though. It was as though he had to
know everything. He became fluent in nine languages. Most
of his writing was in Latin, the scholarly language of his day.
As incidental hobbies he learned bookbinding, watchmaking,
cabinetmaking, instrument making, engraving, marble inlay,

lens grinding, mechanics, and probably other trades. He was no amateur either. The telescope was just being developed, so he ground his own lens and made his own. Anton von Leeuwenhoek was beginning to discover microbes with a primative microscope. Swedenborg couldn't afford to buy one so he made his own. Some friends wanted the printed sheets to make a world globe. When the distributor wouldn't sell these complex forms, Swedenborg designed and engraved his own.

From time to time he developed inventions. Some were crude and interesting ideas for a submarine, a flying machine, and a rapid firing ▆ gun. A working version of his airplane was built and flown in the ▆ nineteenth century. He also worked on more practical things, such as the world's largest drydock, an experimental tank, ▆▆▆, stoves, an ear trumpet, methods of pumping, ▆ fire extinguisher, ▆ musical machine, house heating, and a steel ▆ mill. At one point he directed a project to get small ships fourteen miles over mountains and valleys to help the king win a battle. This doesn't sound like the work of an impractical mystic. He developed more tools than could readily be used or appreciated. Repeatedly he found himself ahead of his time and felt restricted by the conservatism of WOMEN.

In a way all this was just trivia. His real power was in his scientific work. A partial list of his publications will give a sample of his scope:

Date   Title
1. 1714——Inclinations of the Mind
2. 1716——Society of Sciences
3. 1716——Soils and Muds
4. 1716——Fossils
5. 1716——Sailing Upstream
6. 1716——Stereometry
7. 1716——Echo

8. 1717——Causes of Things
9. 1717——Salt Boileries
10. 1717——Tin Work
11. 1717——Stoppage of the Earth
12. 1717——Instituting an Observatory
13. 1717——Commerce and Manufacture
14. 1717——Fire and Colors
15. 1718——Algebra (In his day Swedenborg was the leading mathematician of Sweden.)
16. 1718——To Find the Longitude (This was a major problem then. His was one of the few successful approaches before adequate clocks were developed.)
17. 1718——Welfare of a Country
18. 1718——Essence of Nature
19. 1719——Earth's Revolution
20. 1719——Height of Water
21. 1719——Motive and Vital Essence
22. 1719——Blast Furnaces
23. 1719——Money and Measures
24. 1719——Discovering Mines
25. 1719——Docks, Sluice and Salt Works
26. 1719——Geometry and Algebra
27. 1720——Fall and Rise of Lake Wenner
28. 1721——Indications of the Deluge
29. 1721——Principles of Natural Things, New Attempts to Explain the Phenomena of Chemistry and Physics by Geometry
30. 1721——Iron and Fire
31. 1721——Miscellaneous Observations
32. 1722——Conserving Heat
33. 1722——Working Copper
34. 1722——The Magnet
35. 1722——Calculation Concerning Currency
36. 1722——Hydrostatics
37. 1722——The Genuine Treatment of Metals
38. 1723——Mining Copper and Iron
39. 1723——Establishing Iron Works

40. 1724——On Silver
41. 1724——On Sulphur and Pyrites
42. 1724——On Vitriol
43. 1725——On Salt
44. 1733——Various Philosophical and Anatomical Subjects
45. 1733——Motion of ███ Elements
46. 1733——Empirical Psychology
47. 1734——The Infinite
48. 1734——The Mechanism of the Soul and Body
49. 1734——Human Body
50. 1738——The Infinite and the Finite
51. 1739——Knowledge of the Soul
52. 1740——Muscles in General
53. 1740——Economy of the Soul's Kingdom
54. 1740——The Skin and Tongue
55. 1740——In Celebration of Printing
56. 1740——The Brain (Four volumes and a volume of accurate drawings of the cerebrum.)
57. 1740——Corpuscular Philosophy (Speculations on atomic physics.)
58. 1740——Declination of the Needle
59. 1740——Characteristics and Mathematical Philosophy of Universals
60. 1741——The Fibre
61. 1741——Red Blood
62. 1741——The Five Senses
63. 1741——Action
64. 1742——Rational Psychology
65. 1743——The Generative Organs
66. 1744——Dreams

These represent Swedenborg's 150 early scientific works; they do not include any of his later writings, which his followers consider far more important. There is a pattern to these minor accomplishments. Swedenborg's scientific wanderings tended to lead from the outer material world to the human body and into the psyche. In many instances he summed up all that was known in a particular field and then went to another area. There is a very practical base to his early work. He was interested in processes that enabled men to do things better. He actually worked in all of these areas. He took observations at astronomical observatories, participated in anatomical dissections, etc. He felt he wasn't as good as others at direct observation, i.e., in anatomy. Much of his anatomical work, in which he was one of the foremost masters of his day, was based on the observations of others. His skill was in taking their observations, putting them together into a coherent system, and extracting what the others had not seen. In this way he made several major discoveries in anatomy.

Swedenborg's contributions in the medical sciences, prepared in Latin, lay unnoticed in the library of the Swedish Royal Academy of Sciences until the 1880's, when Tafel translated into English the 4 volume treatise, *The Brain*. Included in this monograph were observations on cortical localizations, the somatropic arrangement of the motor cortex, reference to integrative action of the nervous system, the significance of the pituitary gland, the formation of the cerebrospinal fluid, and a pronouncement on what is now known as the neuron theory. The cerebral cortex, the intermediary between the sensory receptors and the soul, conditions the faculties unique to man such as imagination, judgement, will, and the source of motor volition.

The pituitary gland, the "arch gland" of Swedenborg, was recognized as possessing special function in the body economy, two centuries before contemporary endocrinology. Also, he extended the observations of Willis on the formation of cerebrospinal fluid by the fourth ventricle.[3]

We might add that Swedenborg was also the first to discover the function of the cerebellum. In his understanding of the brain Swedenborg was way ahead of his time. The tireless Emanuel was looking for the soul of man in his anatomical studies. At first he was quite sure he could discover it, but later this hope dimmed. After his experiences in heaven he recognized that the soul was really the life of an individual. He was searching for what was beyond the visible, but he had first to look at the physical basis of man's experience very closely.

In his journey through the sciences he went through the following fields: chemistry, engineering, physics, mathematics, mineralogy, geology, paleontology, anatomy, physiology, astronomy, optics, metallurgy, cosmogony, cosmology, and psychology. It would be difficult to find an area of the science of his day that he hadn't mastered. He can be said to have founded several sciences, such as crystallography.

In his scientific and philosophical works one gets the impression of an immense intellect driven to understand everything. Where microscopes couldn't penetrate, he borrowed analogies from mathematics to speculate on the submicroscopic as he described molecules, atoms and the subatomic. He also struggled mightily to describe the basic, pervasive, integrative principles of creation. Yet he was becoming wary of his ability to reason his way into any realm. There is a brilliant intellectual coldness to his later scientific works, and a feeling that he was perhaps reaching too far. Yet, as in the above anatomical works, his reach sometimes described findings one and two centuries ahead of his time. For anyone who has seen the clear, sure ease and beauty of his later works, these early scientific works have the sad quality of a lonely, brilliant man working tirelessly to reason out all of nature's secrets.

At fifty-six, Swedenborg had mastered all known natural science and stood at the door of psychology. Consider his life at this time. He was now moderately wealthy, especially for a man of simple tastes. He had a half pension from the Board of Mines and earnings from publications and mining investments.

He built a small estate on the outskirts of Stockholm. On a large lot there were several small structures, a barn, and a large garden decoratively laid out. Later he had built a wooden maze for the entertainment of visitors and especially their children. He also built a clever triangular house on the northern edge of his land. It had three double doors and three corner windows. When all of the doors were opened and a mirror was placed in front of a fourth wall along a board fence, "Three gardens are seen reflected in it, in which everything is represented as in the same order as in the original garden." [4] In addition there was a bower for birds. Swedenborg lived here whenever he was in Sweden. He had a gardener who planted vegetables and lime trees and whose wife was the housekeeper. Carl Robsahm, a treasurer of the Stockholm Bank, later described Swedenborg's situation.

Swedenborg's property was about a stone's cast in length and in breadth. The rooms of his dwelling-house were small and plain; but were sufficient for him, though scarcely for anyone else. Although he was a learned man, no books were ever seen in his room, except his Hebrew and Greek Bible, and his manuscript indexes to his own works, by which, in making quotations, he was saved the trouble of examining all that he had previously written or printed.

Swedenborg worked without much regard to the distinction of day and night, having no fixed time for labour or rest. "When I am sleepy," he said, "I go to bed." All the attendance he required from his servant, his gardener's wife, consisted in her making his bed, and placing a large jug of water in his anteroom, his house-keeping being so arranged that he could make his own coffee in his study; and this coffee he drank in great abundance day and night, and with a great deal of sugar. When not invited out, his dinner consisted of nothing but a roll soaked in boiled milk; and this was his meal always when he dined at home. He never at that time used wine or strong drink, nor did he eat anything in the evening; but in company he would eat freely, and indulge moderately in a social glass. . . .

I must also mention a blind door which he had made; and when this was opened, another one appeared with a window in it; and as both these doors were directly opposite a green hedge where a beautiful bird cage was placed, and as the window in the inner door was made of looking-glass, the effect was most charming and surprising to those who opened it with a view of entering Swedenborg's other garden, which, according to his statement was much more beautiful than his first one. Swedenborg derived much sport from this arrangement, especially when inquisitive and curious young ladies came into his garden.

Before his house there was an ornamental flower bed upon which he expended considerable sums of money; he had there even some of those singular Dutch figures of animals, and other objects shaped out of box-trees; but this bed he did not keep up in his later years. The cultivation of the garden, however, and its produce he left to the gardener.

The fire in the stove of his study was never allowed to go out, from autumn, throughout the whole of winter, until spring; for as he always needed coffee, and as he made it himself, without milk or cream, and as he had never any definite time for sleeping, he always required to have a fire.

His sleeping room was always without fire; and when he lay down, according to the severity of the winter, he covered himself either with three or four woolen blankets; but I remember one winter, which was so cold that he was obliged to move his bed into the study.

As soon as he awoke, he went into his study,—where he always found glowing embers—put wood upon the burning coals, and a few pieces of birchrind, which for convenience he used to purchase in bundles, so as to be able to make a fire speedily; and then he sat down to write.

. . . His dress in winter consisted of a fur coat of reindeer skin, and in summer of a dressing-gown; both well worn, as became a philosopher's wardrobe. His wearing apparel was simple, but neat. Still, it happened sometimes, that, when he prepared to go out, and his people did not call his attention to it, something would be forgotten or neglected in his dress; so that, for instance, he would put one buckle of gems and another of silver in his shoes; an instance of which absence of mind I myself saw at my father's house, where he was invited to dine; and which occurence greatly amused several young ladies. Docs I, p. 31

Then, he started out on what were to be his boldest and greatest discoveries. It was as though all his prior work was just a prelude, a preparation, and in later years he said as much. His persistent search for the soul had taken him through anatomy and physiology to the door of psychology. With his usual thoroughness he surveyed and summarized all that was then known of psychology.[5] In the mid-eighteenth century psychology had not yet fully emerged as a separate discipline. It was a mixture of philosophy, religion, and comments on moral matters. There was little direct grasp of inner experience. Swedenborg dutifully searched out the wisdom of Aristotle, Plato, and other wise ones down to his time. For over a century after Swedenborg, psychology was destined to remain faculty psychology. That is, the inner life was divided into faculties such as memory, rationality, avarice, will, etc., and then men would speculate on the interactions between these faculties. The resultant psychology sounded like a dull philosophical tome. For instance, before his enlightenment, Swedenborg described sexual relations in this dull, overly intellectual way:

The act of venereal love is the actual conjunction and union of two bodies into one. Its most deeply laid up cause is drawn from the soul and the pure intellectory, which regard effects not as effects but as ends. Their ends are the existence of society and the procreation of its members. . . . The rational mind is what perceives and understands these ends, partly from itself and partly from things revealed; the animus merely desires the effect; and the body carries it out. How great is the desire of this end in the soul and the pure intellectory is manifestly apparent from the delights of the body and its incitements to this effect. RP 204

Here he described sexual relations from the viewpoint of reason. It was as though reason was taken as the real nature and substance of all mental experience and reason would rationalize the odd doings within the mind and body. This kind of thinking very much reflected his day.

Swedenborg was probably unaware that he took a great step when he tried to describe mental experience directly. From his standpoint the decision was natural enough. He had collected facts from every other area. Why not try to penetrate inward and observe the operations of the psyche directly? Perhaps he could catch the soul at work. And he did. This study is now called phenomenology. It gathers the raw data of experience itself and attempts to observe, understand, and describe human experience itself. As in many other things Swedenborg was ahead of his time. In 1744 he dutifully started recording and interpreting his dreams. He had occasionally set down dreams as far back as 1736, but these occupied just a couple of pages now lost. When his relatives saw the nature of these early dreams they tore them out of his notebook. They probably looked too revealing. The general public hadn't examined or faced up to the saucy nature of average dreams. From this time on Swedenborg very systematically set down dreams and inner experiences in what became his *Journal of Dreams* and his five-volume *Spiritual Diary.*[6] Neither of these were ever intended for publication, for they were the personal notebooks of an inward explorer. They are of tremendous value because they detail the path he was going over—the path on which he almost found too much. When the *Journal of Dreams* was published after his death it caused some sensation. The inner struggles of a man were laid bare. Even his sexual needs were apparent. His followers were caught between scholarship and the need to serve Swedenborg's interests. While most dreams were translated for all to read, the sexual ones were discreetly hidden in Latin.

The dreams and the *Spiritual Diary* were written at a time when his life was changing radically. The super intellect was going inward to find the wellspring of the psyche. He was greatly changed by this. There is hardly any comparison between his writings before and after this period. Before this he was a dry, proper, brilliant, and somewhat proud intellect. After this he was a humble man of great human feeling. He retained the need to order and explain all things, but he now cut to the heart of the human situation with remarkable incisiveness. The scientist became the mystic after he looked within. There followed such a complex series of visions and disturbed psychic experiences that many of Swedenborg's followers are not sure but that he really went mad. Many of those who are very taken by the beauty and richness of his later works are bothered by the mixture of strange experiences that crowd his private journals as he went within.

But what of Swedenborg's outer life as he began to bend his talent for investigation to the sources of mind itself? As numerous acquaintances and documents suggest, his outer life remained quite normal. He was a brilliant nobleman who enjoyed traveling, looking at things and places, and meeting new people. A bit of his private travel notes dated 1739 and 1743 gives some impression:

On the 8th they had horse races; on the 9th racing in chariots; on the 14th pugilistic matches, for which handsome prizes were appointed.

March 14. I left Leghorn [Italy] for Genoa in a felucca; on the way we were in great fear of the Algerines.

March 17. I arrive in Genoa; it has a beautiful harbor, splendid palaces of Balbi, Negro, Doria, and others. I saw the government building and also handsome paintings, where I found more living persons represented than I had seen before; likewise the monument of Columbus, who was a Genoese. I saw the doge, who is always in red down to the very shoes . . . Docs II, p. 129

August 12. I arrived at Hamburg and took lodgings at the Kaiserhof, where the Countess De la Gardie likewise stayed. I met Baron Hamilton, Reuterholm, Trievald, Konig . . . and was presented to Prince Augustus, the brother of His Majesty, who spoke Swedish; afterwards I was presented by Lesch, the marshal in chief, to His Royal Highness Adolphus Frederic; I submitted to him the contents of the book [*The Animal Kingdom*] which I am about to have printed, and showed him the review , of the former work.

August 17. I left Hamburg, and after crossing the Elbe, came to Buxtehude. I there saw, to the extent of a German mile, the most charming country I have yet seen in Germany, having passed through a continuous orchard of apple, pear, plum, walnut, chestnut trees, limes and elms. Docs II, p. 132

He enjoyed travel. Everywhere he examined interesting settings, major buildings and libraries, and he met prominent people. It is said he never turned down a dinner invitation, turning up in one of his two dress suits. He personally knew most of the prominent scientists of his time. His journeys took him from Stockholm to Paris, Amsterdam, and London, and back to Stockholm repeatedly. His voluminous writings made it necessary to take lodgings near his printers. Even when his handwriting was fast and careless the Dutch printers could read it. He had to prepare a clean copy of every book for the printer written in his tiny handwriting with a quill pen. Then there was the task of correcting galley proofs and the numerous business details of his works, which were appearing in several languages.

As the years wore on his habits seem to have become simpler. The man who earlier recorded being introduced to various noblemen and kings would take six shilling a week lodgings in London. His study of inner experiences and writing took most of his time. When asked how he could write so much, he casually said his angel dictated to him and he could write fast enough (Docs III, p. 1017). A number of eyewitnesses heard him calling out to God when alone or speaking to invisible figures. His servant learned not to

bother the master when he was busy with these higher matters. Yet he could be interrupted deep in the midst of a trance
and with little hesitation deal with a startled visitor. He must
have enjoyed beautiful visions. When he completed one religious work he saw "the angelic heaven from the east to the
west, and from the south to the north, appeared of a deep
scarlet color with the most beautiful flowers" (Docs III, p.
1008).

Though he concealed his rich inner life for many years,
accidental demonstrations of his now extraordinary powers,
often at social gatherings, gradually let the world know that
this was the man who was anonymously publishing such
challenging spiritual books. He was so frank concerning his
spiritual experiences afterward that he easily became the
focus of any social gathering. Even though many of his most
priceless works were sold literally for pennies at his own
expense, recognition of this work came slowly. It wasn't until
people started talking about and being impressed by the
totally new understanding and viewpoints reflected in these
works that denunciation also came to the fore. A very unpleasant experience occurred when he was eighty-one. For a
time some religious leaders in Sweden tried to ban the impor-
tation of his works into Sweden and tried to get him declared
insane. They saw him as a crazy heretic upsetting the state
religion. One simply did not speak of God and heaven and
hell from direct experience, especially when this contradicted
established doctrine. They failed. Swedenborg was too well
known by too many, including heads of states.

Even in his eighties he was described as a vigorous, congenial, sociable gentleman. He had almost no health problems
except for toothaches, which he attributed to the acts of
demons. Nature compensated, for he grew a whole new set
of teeth late in life. It was as though the inner simplicity of
his essential teachings were well reflected in his outer life, for
he spent his last days living with a shopkeeper who sold

chintz, muslin and handkerchiefs in London. The shop-keeper's numerous children favored the old man over their own parents because he never failed to bring them sweets from his walks. In fact, the only thing unusual about him was that he spoke as casually and forthrightly of heaven and hell and their peoples as he could talk of London streets.

His experiences were normal but uncommon. Many others have gone through a similar series. But rarely has anyone so painstakingly described an inward journey. Rarely has such a powerful intellect ever set out to unearth the basis of its own life and experience, and in so doing, stepped through into heaven and hell.

2

Going Within

It is essential to understand how Swedenborg went within, for this is the key to his later findings. His method involves a number of interrelated psychological processes which even today, two centuries later, are not well understood. What is now known of the normal events to be expected from these processes will lend credibility to all his later findings.

Since childhood Swedenborg had a personal practice that happens to be one of the ancient Hindu Yoga and Buddhist ways to enlightenment. He probably didn't know he was following an eastern religious practice because the literature bearing on this had not yet been translated. His method is not surprising in one who so much enjoyed intellectual analysis. He would relax, close his eyes, and focus in on a problem with total concentration. At the same time his breathing would nearly stop. Awareness of the outer world and even bodily sensation would diminish and perhaps disappear. His whole existence would focus on the one issue he wanted to understand.

Bear in mind that he probably had more than the usual power of concentration. A lifetime of seeking answers to great problems had given him much practice. The slowing and limiting of breathing is part of a concentration inward. Simply trying to stop breathing in this state produces anxious reminders of the need for air. First there is the concentration, then the lessened breathing follows. The building up of carbon dioxide in the blood may have something to do with intensifying inner experiences. The problem he was concentrating on would blossom out in new, rich and surprising ways. He first practiced this approach as a child during morning and evening prayers,[7] which probably lent an inner intensity to the meaning of prayer. Judging from his writings, I would guess he stumbled on this method as a child, used it relatively little during his scientific period, and then came back to it when he tried to understand the psyche itself.

In his early fifties (1740–1744) he was finishing several large volumes on anatomy and the brain. It was already becoming apparent to him that he wasn't going to find the soul through anatomical studies. He would have to look at the operations of mind itself. Notice his situation. Other than his self-imposed task of writing there was no work required of him. There was no family to disturb him. He had more than enough income. His servants would help him in his basic needs. He could spend hours and even days in deep thought and meditation. If he lapsed into some inner state his housekeeper and gardener would not bother him. His situation was nearly ideal for one who would explore inward.

He used this intense meditation to penetrate the one matter at hand. At first this approach was hyperintellectual. He adopted a method that would eliminate all matters extraneous to the problem, even breathing. Unknown to him, the method was to bring him to the door of inner processes and change his whole understanding of the mind.

In 1742, while writing on psychology, he described meditation from direct experience. "It follows from the above, that we are able to approach nearer and nearer to the pure intellect [which was his main aim] doing this by means of universal ideas and a kind of passive potency." Passive potency is an attentive receptiveness as in meditation. He felt it was possible to deal with universal ideas, understanding at once all the implications of a thing. This alone suggests considerable practice in this area.

[If] we remove particular ideas, that is, withdraw the mind from terms and ideas that are broken, limited, and material, and at the same time, from desires and loves that are purely natural, then the human intellect, being at rest from heterogeneous throngs, as it were, and remaining only in its own ideas and those proper to the pure intellect, causes our mind to undergo no other changes, or to draw forth no other reasons save those that are concordant with the ideas of the pure intellect. In this way our intellect enjoys inmost repose and inmost delight; for this concurrence then appears as an influx of a certain light of intelligence which illuminates the whole sphere of thought, and, by a certain consensus, I know not whence, draws its whole mind together, and inmostly dictates that a thing is true or good, or that it is false or evil. In this way our intellect is perfected in judgment which grows mature. RP 154

This is the description of an intensely intellectual man who is experienced in using meditation as a distilling and perfecting of thought. Yet this is basically empirical. He is describing what he has repeatedly experienced. As he went further along this path he becames thoroughly empirical. He described what he found even when later dealing with the most insane-sounding events. Though he started this intense meditation as a way of perfecting the intellect of a philosopher, he had stumbled on the value of awakening and describing experience itself. He was a philosopher becoming a phenomenological psychologist. He was bent on finding and describing that he saw.

In meditation, everyone experiences difficulty in keeping his mind on one thought. The following shows that Swedenborg also had difficulty:

In the rational mind are divers loves, and these occupy its whole court and draw it to their sides. . . . In general there are superior loves and inferior loves, the superior being spiritual, and the inferior natural and corporeal. When concentrated in the rational mind, these loves are wont to contend. . . . When our mind has been occupied with profound and long-continued meditation and this is burned out by some corporeal loves, if we then wish to recall to mind things spiritual and more pure, we find this impossible unless the former love with its thought has first been cast out. Such is the case if we wish to call upon God in prayer; we find that the thought can never be pure but is clouded, as it were, and occupied with dense darkness. RP 367

During this period he begins to experience the rare and little-known phenomena called photism. The person who meditates intensely, seeking inner guidance, may find a signal system to guide him. When what he is thinking meets inward approval, the person may suddenly see a flash of light. The light may vary from a pinpoint to a large area, and it is characteristically bright. One normal individual of my acquaintance sees a bright pale blue light signaling correct and a black spot signaling wrong. Some saints report similar experiences. Swedenborg saw an affirming flame. "Such a flame appeared to me so often and, indeed, in different sizes with a diversity of color and splendor, that during some months when I was writing a certain work, hardly a day passed in which a flame did not appear as vividly as the flame of a household hearth. It was a sign of approval." WE 6905

Some might confuse this with explosions of light seen by people with migraine or other minor cerebral conditions. Swedenborg's was a formed image, not random flashes. He had tested out its validity. It was given to affirm that what he was thinking was true. It was also given with a pleasant feeling as though a friend had affirmed a truth.

Swedenborg didn't put a great deal of store by this phenomenon. He only mentions it a few times in his writings. It has several implications though. Swedenborg's inner processes were quite involved in what he was doing and wished to guide him. They could also break forth into consciousness. (We will see later that much more was to come.) Last, there is a symbolism even in the fact that it was a flame he saw. The flame, both by its color and warmth, symbolizes love and feeling. Though his was still a ponderous intellect, it was very much love and feeling that were to come forth later. It was another and a rare sign that he was opening up inner processes.

What Swedenborg began as an intense, intellectual form of meditation opened out into an exploration of the hypnogogic state, dreams, and, later, trances. This is a usual series of discoveries as one goes inward. Few can reach the trance level he reached, where the breathing almost stops. I would like to emphasize the normal findings in meditation and the hypnogogic state, experiences available to anyone who troubles to seek them and are relatively simple and harmless. The trance is another matter. The phenomena anyone can find in meditation and the hypnogogic state amply illustrate the path Swedenborg was exploring and give normal individuals samples of the kind of discoveries he was making. Swedenborg seems far less strange to those who bother to look at the same area of human experience.

Very few people have practiced meditation or looked at the hypnogogic experience, so it would be useful to elaborate on the usual things one can expect. I stress usual. Everyone will have roughly the same findings, though the symbolism that emerges may differ. In some ways the reader may have to experience these states to appreciate what they have to teach. They are described in more detail in my book, *The Natural Depth in Man.*[8]

In meditation, first the mind wanders off. It takes practice to stay focused. Like a restless beast the mind jumps to an itch, distracting noises, random thoughts, worries, etc. The original problem vanishes many times. Just a little work of this kind teaches the meditator that he isn't in control of his mind. The effort to call the mind back sets up an internal split: the person trying to concentrate and a host of other odds and ends appearing. The observant person may be beguiled into one of these mental perambulations only to find later that he wandered off into a dream and sleep. Zen monks doing this same sort of thing sit up with eyes fixed on a spot to prevent sleep. It takes practice to tame the restless inner beast and not be carried off by it.

Next the observer learns to watch inner processes. Much that disturbed the meditator earlier was the first surfacing of these inner processes. The observer watches feelings, ideas, faint images, words, sentences, and later whole scenes come and go. He is watching mental processes occur spontaneously. It is common that the observer, seeking inner events, overreacts upon seeing or hearing something. This overalertness tends to knock out the spontaneous processes emerging from the psyche, which are delicate and faint at first. A balance needs to be learned between the responding observer and spontaneous phenomena that turn up. At this level the original meditation has deepened into the hypnogogic state.

The hypnogogic state is one that is usually experienced by everyone twice a day, going into and out of sleep. Few people ever pause at this level to explore the spontaneous wellsprings of mind bubbling forth. This state is a delicate balance of self-awareness and the presence of inner processes. If caught up in the inner processes one can be swept away into a dream and sleep. The same symbolism that appears in dreams appears in the hypnogogic state. But one can't normally talk to or deal with dreams. There is enough self-awareness in the hypnogogic state to remember, record, and even talk to inner processes. This makes it a much more fruitful area for one who wishes to explore inward and even experiment with inner processes.

Swedenborg explored the hypnogogic state more than anyone else has before or since. Yet most of the time he appeared to have gone beyond it into a trance. In the trance inner experiences are no longer delicate and faint, but are clear, intense, and real. Personal awareness still exists, but bodily awareness is less or lost altogether. Many people have been frightened by falling into a trance while going to sleep. Suddenly there is a feeling of intensified consciousness but a paralysis of the body. The frightened person fights to regain control of his body and awaken again. He has to go through a long inner training to reach and learn to be comfortable in this inner state. The hypnotic state is probably closely related to the trance. In hypnosis one is talked into and controlled by the hypnotist; in a trance the subject controls himself. To be able to induce a trance and stay in it implies a great deal of learning and inner experience.

Since many fear inner states, it may be necessary to dispose of their relationship to madness or psychosis. Psychotic hallucinations are probably the spontaneous eruption into consciousness of trance and dreamlike material, implying that consciousness is weakened. In contrast to the capable seeker who deliberately enters a trance, the psychotic usually does not seek and cannot control the eruption of this material into awareness. There is probably a high correlation between the content of psychotic hallucinations and trancelike material. The difference is an impaired ego, not understanding or wanting these processes, as against a healthy ego seeking to evoke inner processes. Quite possibly exploration of these states could prevent madness because they give the individual keys to understanding what bothers him.

For the present let us deal primarily with the hypnogogic state since it is more widely known and experienced than the deeper trances that Swedenborg explored even more extensively. It is curious that the hypnogogic state is still little known. There are many psychologists who know little of its existence, let alone its nature; Jean-Paul Sartre explored it.[9]

On the way into sleep one goes through a stage in which there is still some awareness of the self relaxing and the spinning out of inner ideas, fantasies, words or scenes. Similarly, on awakening in the morning, one can linger on the edge of inner imagery-fantasy while being partially awake. Those who really explore this state can linger for hours watching scenes and hearing things said. For unknown reasons some people are primarily auditory, or hear things in this state, while others primarily see things. The deeper one goes into this state the more likely the experience will be both auditory and visual.

Herbert Silberer, writing two centuries after Swedenborg, noticed that this state is autosymbolic.[10] That is, whatever is true of the individual at that moment tends to be spontaneously represented or symbolized. For instance, I was meditating on the richness of the hypnogogic state and heard someone say "my liberal arts course." The liberal arts course is a representation of my feeling that the inner is varied and informative. I did not have the idea of liberal arts course in mind at that moment. Hence the comment is not immediately understood. These symbolic representations come as a surprise, precisely like listening to someone else who thinks symbolically. This autosymbolic character is a real secret of this process. After looking at the process for months Sartre failed to notice this correlation. The inner can represent fleeting feelings or ideas so fast that the observer is hard put to recall what the feeling was a moment afterward.

Silberer gives a number of examples of this spontaneous symbolism from the hypnogogic state. He is using it to meditate on a problem much as Swedenborg did.

"I think of human understanding probing into the foggy and difficult problem of the 'mothers' (*Faust,* Part II).

"Symbol: I stand alone on a stone jetty extending out far into a dark sea. The waters of the ocean and the dark and mysteriously heavy air unite at the horizon.

"Interpretation: The jetty in the dark sea corresponds to the probing into the difficult problem. The union of air and water, the elimination of the distinction between above and below, should symbolize that, with the mothers, as Mephistopheles describes it, all times and places shade into each other so that there are no boundaries between here and there, above and below. It is in this sense that Mephistopheles says to Faust: 'Now you may sink!—I could just as well say: rise.'

"I decide to dissuade someone from carrying out a dangerous resolution. I want to tell him, 'If you do that, grave misfortune will befall you.'

"Symbol: I see three gruesome-looking riders on black horses storming by over a dusky field under leaden skies."

A host of experiences is possible in this state. One can watch feelings arise and gradually clarify themselves into phrases or sentences or scenes. It immediately becomes apparent that the mind can think without any apparent effort. In fact, without the interference of the little self, it thinks faster, clearer, and more richly. For instance, I was half asleep in the morning and sleepily watched the inner process. It was coming and going as I rose out of sleep and then fell back again. I lapsed into a feeling of understanding. Suddenly I heard "between, I heard the understood." "Between" in a single word captures this coming and going process. "I heard" reflects that the experience is primarily auditory. "I heard the understood" reflects back that I am hearing words that reflect the feeling of understanding. The order of the phrase is correct too. I heard, then I understood. That is, hearing this sentence comes before its understanding. In ordinary thinking one can feel and anticipate what is coming next. In the hypnogogic something is said or seen before there is any possibility of understanding what it means. One can have many of these inner experiences that are difficult to understand at all. For instance I heard "anzeema." The best I could guess was that this name accurately represented feelings, but the feeling and how it matched the word was lost. It is also characteristic of this state that a great deal is artfully condensed into a sentence or a scene. Whatever the source of this process, it seems to think with lightning speed in a rich, symbolic way.

One morning while slowly waking I saw a striking painting. It was done in somber tones of gray, blue, and black and depicted a rough landscape rising from plains on the left to rough rocky mountains on the right. Dramatically superimposed on the center of the painting was a rounded black number 5. The feeling was peaceful and yet powerfully mystical. The whole painting seemed terribly impressive. I have many associations, yet the meaning is far from clear. From the depths came a painting representative of me and yet it said more than I could immediately grasp. It was momentous and portentous of I know not what. The whole hypnogogic state has this characteristic, as though one is dealing with what lies over the edge of consciousness and the understanding.

Swedenborg described the hypnogogic state thus:

But different is the vision which comes when one is in full wakefulness, with the eyes closed. This is such that things are seen as though in clear day. Nay, there is still another kind of vision which comes in a state midway between sleep and wakefulness. The man then supposes that he is fully awake, as it were, inasmuch as all his senses are active. Another vision is that between the time of sleep and the time of wakefulness, when the man is waking up, and has not yet shaken off sleep from his eyes. This is the sweetest of all, for heaven then operates into his rational mind in the utmost tranquility. WE 7387

My experience agrees with his. The hypnogogic experiences while awakening seem to represent tranquility and a deeper understanding than those found on the way into sleep. My painting above is an example.

The following were hypnogogic experiences of Swedenborg's. "I acknowledged that I was impure from head to foot; I cried for the mercy of Jesus Christ. Then it seemed that the words 'I poor sinful creature' occurred to me" (JD 85). This looks clearly autosymbolic. "I heard mentioned the words Nicolaiter, and Nicolaus Nicolai; I do not know if this signifies my new name" (JD 133). Later he comes closer to what it may mean.

"Nicolaus Nicolai was a philosopher who every year sent loaves of bread to Augustus" (SD 134).

The meaning of the comment is hidden in this association. Again, the hypnogogic is speaking from beyond consciousness and its message is not always clear. It sometimes adds a humorous comment as in the following: "Thus as to pleasure, wealth, high position, which I had pursued, I perceived that all was vanity, and that he is the more happy who is not in possession thereof. . . . I seemed to hear a hen cackling, as takes place at once after she has laid an egg" (JD 165). The inner humorously comments on the insight he has just laid. But the chicken is not a very bright animal and she is awfully proud of her new creation. Dumb vanity and pride are being reflected, along with the discovery of creation. Humor in this state is common. It often has this wry character, as though someone is looking down on one's little acts. Like Swedenborg I often wrestle with ultimates. One morning while awakening someone said, "Here is a mondo for you," and I opened my eyes to see the world. A "mondo" is a Japanese Zen term for a problem given by a master to plague the student in a productive way. My higher self was playing with me, saying, "You want a problem from your master? Here is a little one. Existence itself!" It is a joke and serious at the same time, which makes it seriously funny.

One doesn't explore these things for long without beginning to feel there is a greater wisdom in the inner processes than there is in ordinary consciousness. Swedenborg was beginning to trust this inner wisdom: "It seemed as if someone said the words *interiorescit* (he is becoming more internal) and *integratur* (he is being made whole); which signifies that by my infestations I am becoming more purified" (JD 170).

Swedenborg was still working all hours day and night on the last of his anatomical works, while noting down these inner experiences.

This was a Sunday. Before I fell asleep I was deep in thoughts concerning the things on which I am engaged in writing. Then I was told: "Hold your tongue, or I will beat you." I saw someone sitting on a block of ice, and I was frightened. . . . It means that I should not persist in my work so long, especially on a Sunday, or perhaps in the evenings. JD 242

He has to get a message from the beyond to suggest that he shouldn't work on Sunday evenings! At the time he was writing on "Organic Forms in General" in Volume II of *The Animal Kingdom.* Looking at this book, the reader would be inclined to agree with this inner process; he should hold his tongue. He is in a cold, precarious place trying to analyze everything under the sun. The inner threatens to punish him. He is naturally afraid, for it has done so before.

The hypnogogic is just one of a series of inner states that became guides to Swedenborg. Later we will see his dreams, visions, and other numinous experiences. I want to emphasize his meditation and hypnogogic states because they are normal experiences available to anyone, and there are several critical discoveries that anyone who explores these states will make. Swedenborg found them, and they profoundly affected his later thinking. He was, after all, an empirical scientist. He believed what he could concretely see and deal with. I would assert that no one can explore these states in any depth without making the following discoveries which are basic to understanding Swedenborg's later work.

1. *The individual's sphere, in which he rules within his mind, is relatively small.* Waking consciousness normally blocks out the other inner psychic processes. Swedenborg was later to say that it is a gift from God that man even feels that he rules himself. A person cannot spend hours in meditation merely trying to hold his thoughts still without beginning to suspect he isn't master of his own mind. The average person would find it very difficult to steadily hold one thought, image, or intention in mind for one minute. In the hypnogogic state one can watch thoughts form and be spoken without one's behest. Further, the inner process thinks far faster and more cleverly than the meditator and the symbolic language spoken may not even be understood. Those who have explored these states come to feel like a vessel into which life is poured. Moreover, after much watching of thoughts coming forth on their own, one can detect the same process in normal waking consciousness. One learns to recognize auditory hallucinations and other dreamlike processes in normal consciousness. The little fringe thought that pops into one's head in the daytime is no longer seen as one's own creation. It is the same process as occurs near sleep. Only very logical, labored thought feels like one's own, and even here a careful examination will show bursts of intuition and a guidance by background feelings whose source is unknown. Some will be frightened by the idea that there is little that we actually rule in our mind. But this is the normal, common state. We are some kind of coming and going, flowing life process. The main effect of watching this coming and going is a greater humility about how much one is master of, and a greater tolerance for others as their whims come and go. Swedenborg becomes decidedly humble as he goes within and watches these processes. The proud author of many scientific works didn't feel he had the right to put his name

on his psychological-theological works. Through most of his later life these, his greatest works, were issued anonymously. It was too terribly apparent to him that if he did anything of worth, it had been given to him by a power beyond him. This is not a piously assumed humility. It came because he had seen too much formed beyond him and given to him. He saw that even though we are given to feel master of ourselves, any close examination of these inner processes belies this. Life is given to us. What we call ourself is this point of giving.

2. *The capacity to symbolize or represent is a natural one, reflecting some higher understanding within the individual.* For many years Swedenborg explored this symbolic inner capacity. From uncertain beginnings in working out his dreams, he grew into a very rich and sure understanding of this symbolism. A dream symbol could be construed to mean this, that, or anything else depending on one's predilections. In meditation and the hypnogogic the individual can watch symbols form. By looking at feelings, associations, and the situation being autosymbolized, it is possible to penetrate the symbol. These states instruct in the matter of symbolism. One gradually feels that the symbol is the means by which something higher and more inner speaks to the conscious self. It is an intelligent guidance system. Since it is in a higher language than we are accustomed to, the searcher needs to enter into this inner realm to understand its language.

Swedenborg later described this symbolism as correspondences and representations. All orders of existence correspond to each other, just as the expression on his face corresponds to the person's feeling. The lower-level correspondent represents the higher level, just as the facial expression represents the inner mood and feeling. For Swedenborg this is the key to understanding all levels of existence. One couldn't see the present relevance of heaven or hell without this key. It is a difficult key, requiring a certain great intimacy to use it well. One cannot explore these states without beginning to sense the wonder and power of the inner that speaks to one in this higher language.

I was teaching the interpretation of dreams to a counselor. We both sensed her main problem. She was too voluble, spoke easily of anything, but felt little. While passing in the hall she said she dreamed of a poor blind mole in the ground. She could see that she was like the blind mole feeling her way in the dark, but why did he speak Spanish? I said, "Fancy talker your dumb mole," and she saw this representation of her own capacity for fancy talk while she was a lowly blind creature. In this playful, creative way the inner reflects the truth of us. It cannot do otherwise. Jung calls this inner, objective. It can't help but accurately represent. But this truth it represents is greater than our ordinary understanding, hence its language is richer than we are accustomed to.

3. *These inner states raise the issue of the presence of other spiritual beings interacting in our lives.* It is at first disconcerting to hear others speaking inside one's head. But hypnogogic and dream visions aren't so bad. For after all, the mind that visualizes might go on picturing things even when the eyes aren't in use. But people talking, saying things not wholly understood, gives one the feeling of the presence of other beings. I stress that these auditory hallucinations are quite normal and common in this state. They differ from psychotic hallucinations not so much in content but in the circumstances. The psychotic hallucination occurs in a disturbed person in the waking state and is clear and distinct. Hypnogogic hallucinations are delicate, faint, and require a very inward state with little ego awareness to even awaken them.

Times have changed since Swedenborg explored these areas. His father, the bishop, had heard and seen angels. It was part of his calling. During Swedenborg's time there was a rash of spirit possession in Sweden. When he heard and saw things he naturally thought of spirits. Now we experience the same phenomena and think they must be pieces of the self, bits of the unconscious coming up. For the present I would simply like to leave the issue open. One may be experiencing bits of the self or disincarnate entities, *or* these two may be fundamentally the same thing. Eventually Swedenborg sees them as the same thing. Other lives are unconscious parts of our own life. It is enough for the present to say experiences in these states suggest the presence of spirits interacting in our innermost feelings.

It was said later that Swedenborg the scientist changed into a mystic. This isn't quite true. Swedenborg the empirical scientist remained a scientist reporting his findings even when he went within. It is just that he took an unusual and direct path to the underpinnings of human experience itself, stirring up findings that still need explaining. The essential pattern of his findings is already implied at this level. The rest of the journey inward was not so easy, for he entered into a mighty struggle with inner forces.

It might be asked whether it was an advantage or disadvantage for Swedenborg to explore inward long before psychology and psychoanalysis came along to "explain everything." It was a disadvantage in that he described what so few understood. But an advantage was that he had no chaos of theories or opinions to distort his vision. He could describe things just as he found them. He even felt that divine guidance suggested he shouldn't read the theologies of others. They would introduce too many errors for him to work through. Being among the first to really explore the inner landscape, without the guidance of theories, he was thrown back on describing things just as he found them. He felt free to look at what the later morass of theory would suggest he should avoid. In a fundamental way he had chosen to examine inner processes in the most direct way possible.

3

Opening the Inner World

In 1744 Swedenborg was still working on the last of his scientific works. His four volumes on the brain were a brilliant breakthrough, throwing light on operations of the brain that can only be appreciated centuries later. He was also doing a very perceptive, though still rather intellectual, work on psychology. His outer life was eminently successful and productive. Yet he had failed in his quest to find the soul through science. This quest was more serious and important than anyone would have guessed. In a kind of middle-life crisis he was called away from his outer success to attempt the impossible through the inner search. He had a taste of the inward journey, and he took this up more and more seriously. In his intense meditation, he began to find deeper processes. Symbols arose. Instead of just occasionally jotting down dreams, he began to record and interpret them daily.

Almost by accident his *Journal of Dreams* has come down to us. He wrote many things he did not intended to publish, and this was one of them. Being a personal journal, he was quite honest with himself. The first dream notes are brief, but they imply a struggle that will become more apparent.

In Leipzig, about the one who lay in seething water.

About the one who tumbled with the chain into the depth. JD 4–5

I was standing by a machine which was moved by a wheel; its spokes involved me more and more and carried me up so that I could not escape: I awoke. It signifies either that I need to be kept further in the dilemma, or else that it concerned the lungs in the womb, on which subject I then wrote immediately afterwards; both. JD 18

For the reader who has examined dreams, these are not unusual. They reflect some inner stress but of normal extent. As he went inward he was being carried up as though by a machine. He was not sure of the direction and hence didn't feel safe. Since his thinking and writing occupied his whole life, it is not surprising that he related dreams to this. The wheel's shape may well have been associated with fetal lungs for him. But he wisely saw a deeper meaning. He was being carried along in a dilemma. We can only guess at its meaning. Above all else he wanted to know what was true. But in these dreams he sensed he was being carried off in some unknown direction in a world of strange fancies. Later he found that the lungs and respiration have to do with understanding. His fetal understanding became more and more involved and carried up by this inner process; he could no longer escape from it.

Other dreams comment on some sort of impurity in himself.

I was in a garden containing many fine beds, one of which I desired to own, but I looked about to see if there was any road to walk out; I also seemed to see, and thought of another; there was one there who was picking away a heap of invisible vermin and killed them; he said they were bedbugs which some person had carried thither and thrown in, infesting those who were there. I did not see them, but some other little insect, which I dropped on a white linen cloth beside a woman; it was the impurity which ought to be rooted out of me. JD 19

A paraphrase of this dream (and any dream) helps reveal its meaning. "I want something nice and beautiful. I see an escape but I am ambivalent about which way to go. There are invisible vermin around. I am responsible for some of the impurity which is associated with a woman."

King Charles was sitting in a dark room and said something, but somewhat indistinctly. He afterwards closed the windows, and I helped him with the curtains. Afterwards I mounted a horse, but did not take the road I had intended but went across hills and mountains, riding swiftly. A wagon with a load followed after me, and I could not get away from it; still the horse by the load became tired, and the driver wanted to get into some place; he came in, and the horse became like a slaughtered, bloody beast, fallen down. JD 31

In paraphrase, "A higher being can't get through to me. He and I close off the light. I am not going the way I intended. Though fast, I pull such a load as to kill me." He was still working hard on his scientific writing, and he pulled such a load. The higher one hadn't gotten through to him, and the light was shut out. His own interpretation conformed closely to this.

The dreams at this time were trying to pull him away from his excessive intellectual and scientific work. Though mildly complimentary, they said it really was a heap of rubbish. He partly missed and partly saw this message. He also felt full of vermin, filth, unworthiness. He knew he needed help, but he only partly saw it coming. He was very religious; this whole process was cast in a religious framework. There was evil in him that should be rooted out. But how? He had very much shut off his own feelings, and in dreams he didn't get along well with women, who represent feelings. He was wary of women-feelings. Maybe they would lead him astray.

Most of us live so far from an age in which one fights evil temptations that it is worth commenting on this as a psychological process. To fight evil temptations sounds precisely like trying to repress and deny a part of the self. It seems like the opposite of integrating these tendencies. Actually, it is integrative in its own way. The one fighting temptations becomes very much aware of his other side; one can't fight demons for long without feeling how alive they are in one's self.

When these dreams were first published after his death, Swedenborg's detractors leapt on his sexual dreams as though they showed he was some sort of sex fiend. I would like to deal with this sexual side, for it bears directly on the central drama of his struggles. It also illuminates how fighting temptations can help integrate the other side of one's self. Also, in the sexual aspects of his dreams his humanness shows particularly well.

Swedenborg's early detractors surely had not looked at their own dreams, for they would have seen much more of sex than Swedenborg shows in his *Journal of Dreams.* Out of some 250 dreams, nine—comparatively few—show a recognizable sexual theme. It is in accord with his statement early in the *Journal,* "I wondered . . . how the inclination for women, which had been my chief passion, so suddenly ceased" (JD 14). This former passion for women comes as something of a surprise to anyone who pursued his earlier history and writings, for it wasn't apparent. There were hints that he had arranged his life so he didn't see women alone. Now in his fifties, passion was calming down. More than this, it could well be that the need for women was in effect the feeling side saying, "Relax, live, enjoy yourself as other men do." But his life-style was relatively Spartan, self-denying and self-demanding. It could also be that his passion for women finally diminished because he was clearly going within. He was going to meet feeling in all her forms, and so didn't need the external attraction to call him back to feeling.

The earliest sexual dream represented the difficulty he was having with his soft feeling side.

I stretched out alongside of one who, although she was not beautiful, nevertheless appealed to me. In the spot where I touched her she was like others in front but there was something like teeth. To Archenholtz it seemed to be a female shape. What is meant I do not know—whether to keep one's tongue [be silent] in matters of state, whether anything. JD 120

Swedenborg was puzzled, as well he might be. The idea of the *vagina dentata,* the vagina with teeth, was something psychoanalysts were to run into much later. The same theme turned up again in dream 261. A paraphrase will clarify what is involved: "I am relaxing alongside something soft and pleasant. It attracts me though it isn't beautiful. I want to join with this softness, but I cannot be comfortable with it. We (I am) are in doubt about what it is." We can't be sure of Swedenborg's associations with his friend Johan Archenholtz. Like Swedenborg, this man had opposed Sweden going to war with Russia and had been tortured for his beliefs. Archenholtz, one who was ready to suffer for his beliefs, seemed to think it was a female form. Swedenborg, another ready to suffer for his beliefs, was attracted to soft, warm, feeling, but he couldn't get along with it. This theme turns up repeatedly in the dreams. He was not against love-women-feeling, but he had not come to terms with it yet. He was struggling mightily to put down sex-feeling-corporeal thoughts. Right after the only clear sexual intercourse dream this follows:

"Afterwards I slept a little, and it appeared to me as if there was flowing a quantity of oil with a little mustard mixed with it. This may signify my life that is coming, and it may mean pleasantness mixed with adversity, or it may mean a medicine for me." JD 173

After sex, oil flows, which signifies something sensual, smooth, and pleasant. But it is mixed with something sharp in taste. Feeling has been released in the inner world, but with it comes a little note of warning, the mustard seed. We have the advantage of seeing all the subsequent events. He was correct; he was to know pleasantness mixed with adversity. This was his medicine, designed by this inner process.

The next night this dream appeared:

> During the whole night, for about eleven hours, I was in a strange trance, neither asleep nor awake. I knew all that I dreamt, but my thoughts were kept bound, which at times caused me to sweat. I cannot describe the nature of that sleep, during which my double thoughts were as it were separated from each other or torn asunder. JD 174

(One of the quickest and surest ways to awaken the inner life is to deny bodily pleasure. This is probably why visions are rare these days.) He fell into a trance. He could not control his thoughts. Doubling of thought is relatively rare: each thought arises with its own opposite and there is opposition. The mental sphere is torn apart with the energy generated. One is primarily experiencing feeling; thought is a helpless pawn. The world of feeling explodes internally and tears apart thought. There is no safe refuge for the beset person. He hangs on, hoping to weather the storm. Swedenborg was indeed to experience pleasantness mixed with adversity. On both scores, pleasantness and adversity, he was being educated in the world of feeling. If he had just relaxed and lived out his sexual needs, this would have been much less likely to happen. His heroic combat against passion and ▉ corporeal temptations meant that he was going to experience more feeling than most. The *Spiritual Diary,* which followed the *Journal,* is shot through with awesome feeling and experience. The cold, clear intellect that would retreat to a block of ice was being melted by its own heroic effort to find the real truth.

> A married woman wanted to have me, but I liked an unmarried one; the former one became angry and persecuted me, but I nevertheless gained the unmarried one and was with her and loved her.

It was a woman who owned a very beautiful estate in which we walked about, and I was to marry her. She signified (piety) and also, I believe, wisdom, which owned these possessions. Also when I was alone with her I loved her for high-minded character which it seemed she possessed ▨ by herself. (JD 178–179)

Paraphrase: "I reject the improper, so it torments me. I accept and love the greatness of what is beautiful and proper. With this I can join."

His struggle against corporeal feeling and temptation awakened an assault of feeling. He was coming to terms with feeling. He could accept what was proper and would reject what seemed improper. He was involved in a personal analysis, as at least one analyst noticed.[11] This is the way analysis should go. The individual chooses what is right and proper for him. If he simply accepts everything that comes from within, he dissolves in the depth and becomes its pawn. He is no longer cutting off feeling, he is merely driving it to a higher level of sublimation. For instance, in Kundalini Yoga, the root of life is represented by a serpent that lives coiled at the base of the spine. If this serpent is allowed to easily escape as sexual impulse, which is handy to where he lives, the yogi doesn't discover his higher possibilities. The snake simply appears as a sex drive. The adept becomes very aware of the serpent Kundalini and forces him to rise up the spine. If he must get out, it will be at the highest level, the mind. As Kundalini escapes out of the mind, it shatters the individual's conventional ideas of reality and the serpent has become the Divine itself. This possibility could not be discovered unless all the lower escapes were blocked. By wrestling with corporeal thoughts and evil temptations, Swedenborg generated a tense struggle to instruct him on the power and reality of feeling. By accepting only the highest aspect of feeling, he was driving it to show him its highest possibilities. Kundalini is to escape only through his mind.

It is characteristic of a dream series or a personal analysis that the person doesn't show a simple linear progress. The line of progress is much more complex, like a spiral that shows cyclic ups and downs during a gradual rise of the overall trend. The 286 entries in the *Journal of Dreams* show such a progress. Many times Swedenborg sensed himself as unworthy or ignorant, yet the level of his understanding gradually increased. From a first, halting use of symbols, he became very accustomed to this language and could even describe himself in symbolic terms. Over and over the theme of temptation reappears. It means he had awakened some inner potentiality and had to struggle with its power, while he became more powerful. At times he describes this process as infestation—a struggle with alien forces opposed to the individual: "While I was in the first infestation I cried to Jesus for help, and it went away, I also kept my hands folded under my head, and then it did not return a second time. I was nevertheless in tremors when I awoke, and now and then I heard a dull sound, but I do not know whence it came" (JD 98).

The tremors imply that the inner forces are strong and the controls are taxed. The struggle is very real. It even has a physical side to it. He referred to swoons and fainting fits (JD 282). This is no minor intellectual struggle. Double thoughts were reported several times. In these he would experience thought and its opposite without control. This was part of the enlivening of the whole sphere. It was also part of the medicine he needed, to learn that he couldn't control everything.

Then he also had periods of ecstasy.

I had a preternaturally good and long sleep for twelve hours. On awakening I had before my eyes Jesus crucified and His cross. The spirit came with its heavenly and, as it were, ecstatic life so intensely, and permitting me to enter into it higher and higher, so that, if I had gone still higher, I would have been dissolved by this veritable life of joy. JD 127

The ecstatic respites between storms assured him he was on the right track. The storms were like seas of feeling tossing him about, teaching him his smallness. His pride in his own powers became less and less. There were several experiences of God. He suspected from the beginning that the higher, wiser, symbolic power within him might stem from God. This poor, beset vessel of a man had several confirming experiences that encouraged him to go on with his terrible struggle. They came from ▮▮ directions—they were ▮▮ just dream experiences. The following clearly shows the respite quality of these religious experiences; it is also a complex of experiences.

At ten o'clock I went to bed and felt somewhat better. Half an hour afterwards I heard a noise beneath my head and I then thought that the tempter had departed. Immediately there came over me a powerful tremor, from the head and over the whole body, together with a resounding noise, and this occurred a number of times. I found that something holy had encompassed me. I then fell asleep, but about twelve, one or two o'clock in the night there came over me a very powerful tremor from head to the feet, accompanied with a booming sound as if many winds had clashed one against another. It was indescribable, and it shook me and prostrated me on my face. In the moment that I was prostrated I became wide awake, and I saw that I had been thrown down. I wondered what it meant, and I spoke as if I were awake, but still I found that the words were put into my mouth, and I said, "Oh, thou almighty Jesus Christ, who of thy great mercy deignest to come to so great a sinner, make me worthy of this grace!" I kept my hands folded and I prayed, and then there came forth a hand which strongly pressed my hands. . . . In that same moment I was sitting at His bosom and beheld Him face to face. It was a countenance of a holy mien, and all was such that it cannot be expressed, and also smiling, so that I believe that His countenance was such while he lived in the world. He spoke to me and asked if I had a bill of health. I answered, "Lord, thou knowest better than I." He said, "Well, then do." This I found in my mind to signify "Love me truly," or "Do what thou hast promised." JD 51–54

The struggling man finally had a clear confirmation that he was on the right track. It is curious that the Lord spoke to Swedenborg symbolically when He asked about a health certificate. This may have referred in part to an earlier event in Swedenborg's life. He sailed to England at the time that England was desperately fighting the plague, and it was a stormy voyage. He landed without a health certificate, for which the authorities nearly hanged him. So the Lord asks him if he is now clean enough to come ashore from the dangerous sea. Swedenborg no longer presumed to judge his spiritual health. He left it up to the Lord, who answered graciously. The promise was that Swedenborg would give up all his scientific work and devote himself to this inner journey. That is the will of the innermost. He hadn't fully come into compliance with it yet, but he was being prepared for this radical shift in direction. Though intrigued by this inner process, he still set great store by his scientific work. He didn't fully sense that this inner journey would be of such importance that his great scientific work would be like a heap of rubbish in comparison.

This dream occurred not long after the above experience.

Bad dreams, about dogs that were said to be my own countrymen, and which licked my neck but did not bite. . . . In the morning I fell into terrible thoughts, as also during the day, that the Evil One had taken possession of me, yet with the consolation that he was outside and soon would let me go. Just as I was in damnable thoughts, the worst kind that could be, in that very moment Jesus Christ was presented vividly before my internal eyes, and the operation of the Holy Spirit came upon me, so that hence I could know the devil was gone. The next day I was now and then in a state of infestation and in double thoughts and in strife. After dinner I was mostly in a pleasant humor, though engaged in worldly things. Then I traveled to Leyden. JD 167

It is very rare to see a clear mixing of dreams, psychological analysis, and religious processes. The theme of dogs comes up several times in his dreams. If the reader feels what it is like to have an animal licking the neck—a dog that might bite—the meaning can be recovered. The dogs were said to be his countrymen, that is, his associates. Everything in the dream has to be part of himself. Paraphrased, "I have the feeling of some sloppy beast getting near my head." This fits with thoughts of the Evil One possessing him. Yet the danger from the Evil One is only partial. He is outside and will let go. The dog did not bite. Swedenborg was still struggling with his instincts (i.e., his countrymen) that were confounding his thoughts. In the midst of this Christ appeared again, and he was saved. The next day he went about his worldly duties and even made a trip to Leyden, probably to see his scientific works through the press.

Some readers will easily be able to accept that God can be in the midst of the innermost processes of mind. Others will see this as just wishful thinking or some other kind of folly. Whether or not God is there, consider for a moment the psychological value of thinking of the innermost processes in these terms. Whatever is in man is decidedly powerful and very clever. It is powerful enough to overwhelm the individual and destroy him, as in psychosis. Swedenborg later described this process as quite dangerous. The analysts would agree. After one holy tremor or vision, many psychiatrists would be inclined to administer thorazine to dampen down these inner processes. It was quite important that Swedenborg had a set of values and struggled against inner tendencies that he did not consider acceptable. He did not rejoice at every instinct that turned up. Yet his overall feeling toward this outpouring of inner processes was positive. His belief that the inner could contain God had several useful functions. He would look to it as a sincere man searching after God. This meant he would be patient in exploring these processes when most religious people would not have bothered. But along with God there could be other spirits. He would have to sort out the outpourings of this inner region, for not all would be acceptable. Both his scientific attitude and his clear strong personal values helped him in this difficult process. In the eastern religions it is often recommended that one not attempt this exploration until one has reached maturity and most of life's problems are solved. The values of the adolescent are still too fluid to withstand the storm of the inner journey. This is not to say that strong values are not changed by the inward journey, but a set of values, a clear stance in the world, provides a stronger vessel to weather the storm. Whether or not God is within, this provides a suitable approach to the inner. It implies that inside there is great power, wisdom, and danger. God also represents the highest conception of what one hopes to find. Thus Kundalini is driven out of its basement hideout to reach consciousness at the highest possible potentiality. God in the unconscious or in these inner processes also implies change. Things should be very much different and better on reaching this inner potential. ————————————————————————

Swedenborg had several precognitive dreams. Glimpses of one's own future in dreams are not terribly unusual, for most people have such dreams.[12] The difficulty lies in penetrating the symbolism of dreams and then in knowing which ones predict and which merely speak of one's present state. It is curious to see what the dream process would care to tell of Swedenborg's future. "Further, something was told about my book; it was said it would be a divine Book on the worship and love of God; I believe there was also something about spirits; I believe I had something on the subject in my work on the infinite, but there was no reply to that." JD 250

At the time he didn't know it, but shortly after this he started on a book whose title is given in the dream, *The Worship and Love of God.* It was a strange work for him, a flaming example of poetic imagination unlike anything he had ever done before. It was an exercise in a totally new style and conception, making a break with his intellectual work and presaging the soaring quality of his later works. In the dream he wonders if he had not written on this already in *The Infinite and Final Cause of Creation*. The dream didn't answer, but the answer is no. His conception of what the dream was talking about was too limited. It was a totally new work that would rise into consciousness and would have some bearing on spirits.

The next precognitive dream is significant in that it described the most important aspect of his future life. He missed its real meaning altogether, for he could not grasp its predictive quality. Instead, he again thought it referred to a past work.

I beheld the gable end of the most beautiful palace that anyone could see, and the midst of it was shining like the sun. I was told that it had been resolved in the society that I was to become a member, as it were an immortal, which no one had ever been before, unless he had died and lived again: others said that there were several in that state. The thought occurred, whether it is not the most important to be with God and to live. This, therefore, had reference to that which I had just then brought to a finish concerning organic forms in general and especially the conclusion. JD 243

He had some special feeling for the gable end of a palace: he had used the symbol before. It sounds as though the symbol says, "I am in an ideal place." Much of what he reported here as a dream was really a simple statement of fact. It had been resolved in heaven that he could visit. He would be permitted what had been given to no one else before their death. While living, he was to be permitted to visit heaven and hell. The sun in the midst of the palace he would find again in the center of heaven. "[i]t was said there were several in that state"; indeed the several were the multitudes of all that had ever lived. The thought of the importance of being with God was also part of it. In heaven and hell he would know God. The ushering into heaven and hell would take place in several months. His inner search and battles were beginning to pay off. I have no idea why the dream mechanism would bring a nugget like this without also giving the individual the means to understand the precious information. But it happens often. The inner provides ample messages and it is up to the individual to determine their meaning.

There are many signs that Swedenborg was beginning to experience the inner in more than just dreams. The process had become extraordinarily enlivened. Most people who have tried the same practices even on a casual level are inclined to have visions and intense emotional experiences.[13] In Swedenborg this was probably a product of his intense concentration, his yogic practice, his ability to devote himself to these processes, and his great need to encounter the Divine. Most people in personal analysis would prefer to keep the lid on inner processes. But Swedenborg was engaged in a heroic effort toward an encounter with higher inner processes. He was moving about as fast as one could hope in this inner sphere without breaking himself in the process. The main part of the *Journal of Dreams* takes only seven months. Seven years would not be slow for such gains. No wonder the dreams referred to him as getting around fast.

In part, Swedenborg was bent upon bringing these discoveries into his life, though one might have expected a much more detached, intellectual approach to inner processes. He loved real, solid truths. He was rather pleased when a religious vision knocked him off his bed. A later vision that didn't accomplish as much he concluded must have come from lower-order creatures! This was a man who enjoyed grappling with truth. After so many years of thinking and speculating on what was true, it apparently comforted him to be knocked about by lively truths that were greater than he. For this is what he had been looking for, sizable truth, truths as big as life itself. The liveliness of this inner encounter apparently did not scare him as much as it did others, reading of it later, who speculated on his sanity. He was overjoyed at finding truth so real. His main fear was that he was unworthy to advance in this realm, and his battle with feeling or corporeal thoughts was secondary to this.

In addition to several periods of religious ecstacy sprinkled among his inward battles, Swedenborg also experienced several visions. These were simply further signs that the forces he was dealing with were spilling over into his life. The visions occurred relatively late in this dream series. The inner battles were settling and the visions were further guides to him that he was on the way. "On awakening I had a vision, seeing much gold before me, and the air seemed to be full of it. It signifies that our Lord, who disposes all things, provides for me all that I need both as to spiritual and worldly things" (JD 222).This probably occurred in the hypnogogic state. The next dream touches again on the kernal of the problem. "In a vision there appeared as it were a fire of hard coal, burning briskly; it signified the fire of love" (JD 261). A dream followed with the *vagina dentata* in it. The theme of desirable but dangerous to touch was in both the vision of "fire of hard coal, burning briskly," and in the associated sexual image.

I saw also a vision that beautiful loaves of bread were presented to me on a plate. This was a premonition that the Lord Himself will instruct me, since I have now first come into such a state that I know nothing, and that all preconceived opinions have been taken away from me, which is the beginning of learning, viz., that one must first become a child, and then be wet nursed into knowledge, as is now taking place with me. JD 267

It was clear that Swedenborg took seriously the ceremonial use of bread in church. He was honored by this vision of beautiful loaves of bread. He felt he was being instructed by the Lord, the highest bread he could hope for. Though he was really beginning to grasp the whole inner language and trend, he clearly saw himself as ignorant in this sphere. "I know nothing. . . ." Preconceived opinions had been taken away from him. For instance, he no longer related these inner messages to his scientific work. He was in new territory where he was, as it were, an infant being wet-nursed—a soft and feelingful image. He is using the inner symbolic language to describe himself.

"In a vision there appeared a person who was carrying wooden planks; he fell down under the burden, and another person came to help him, but in what manner he was helped up I did not see" (JD 269). It sounds like an image of the struggling Christ—a man carrying planks falls down and is helped. Yet, since it is an image fashioned out of Swedenborg, it must reflect him. He was struggling under a burden that was too much for him, except for unseen help.

The next vision is likely also from the hypnogogic state. It combines two major themes that he had been struggling with in his dreams. "In the morning there appeared to me in a vision a market like the Disting fair; it was in my father's house at Uppsala, in the parlor upstairs, in the entrance, and all over the house" (JD 281). The associations here are too private to be readily understood. The Disting fair was an annual festival held since pagan times in February in Uppsala, Sweden. The fair was dedicated to female deities. The implication is that his difficulty with women-feelings–the corporeal had been settled. From ancient times the mysteries of the feminine had been celebrated, and now it occurs again in Swedenborg. He had been raised in Uppsala, where his main and somewhat limited contact with his austere bishop father took place. That the fair takes place in his "father's house"—and indeed in the parlor and all over the house— implies that it was acceptable to his father. The vision says some kind of joyous acceptance of the feminine had taken place and this would be acceptable to his father. But note that though sex is implied here (female deities) it is on a high plane. The sublimation he strove for in relating to sex-women-feeling had succeeded. He could accept the feminine in terms of its highest implications. Hence he projected in a vision the celebration of female dieties. In several prior dreams he seemed to be working on his differences with his father. His father wanted Emanuel to be a religious man and appeared somewhat disappointed when he chased after the current fad, science. This difference with his father became resolved as Swedenborg gradually turned into an actively religious man.

This same resolution of his struggle with the feminine-feeling aspects of his own inner life shows rather touchingly in his last entry in the *Journal of Dreams.* This time he was just thinking and stating his position. But he was thinking in terms of the symbolism of the inner world and was clearly dealing with delicate feeling. He had come a long way from the rational scientist who set out to find the soul.

Verities or virgins of this kind regard it as shameful to offer themselves for sale; they esteem themselves so precious and dear to their admirers that they show indignation if anyone offers a price, and still more if anyone attempts to purchase them; to others, who hold them vile, they lift their eyebrows. And therefore, lest by the former they should be held beneath valuation, and fall into contempt with the latter, they would rather offer themselves freely to their lovers. I, who am their servitor, would not dare but to obey them, lest I be deprived of their service. JD 286

The idea of verities or truths coming as lovely virgins is a very old one. It goes back to Greek mythology and further. Swedenborg had had a classical education and knew this. The image combines truth and feeling into one. These vestal virgins were within. He was speculating on how one could have one of these women; they couldn't be bought. Moreover, they are not to be seen as just low, sexual seducers—

there is a real danger that these virgins will be misunderstood. The real secret is simple: they give themselves freely to their lover. Swedenborg acknowledged that he was their servant and lover. He could but obey them. The earlier struggle with women-sex-feeling-corporeal thoughts was now resolved. He had found wonder in himself that combined truth and deep feeling. He was a servant of this wonder. All the rest of his writing combined intense feeling and truth, a central theme running all through his discoveries of heaven and hell. He could not have penetrated further unless he had truly accepted his own feeling side.

Many will think—and indeed a Jungian analyst expressed it—that Swedenborg had not really accepted his feeling side.[14] It was too constrained into vestal virgins, lovely repressed images. This is not the usual way of accepting and acting out feelings. I believe firmly that in dealing with the private matters of another man's inner life we should try to understand and accept him *on his own terms*. For instance, this analyst examined the *Journal* and asked if Swedenborg had become integrated in Jungian terms. It did not matter in the least to Swedenborg whether he had become integrated. He was looking for and finding God. This was his whole purpose and the whole measure of success. Also, some would suspect that he merely dodged and displaced his sexual needs by this talk of verities and virgins. Swedenborg chose his own values. He decided to block the lowest bodily expression of feeling that he might find feeling on the highest possible level. This was his choice and where he succeeded. All his subsequent writings were strongly colored by feeling.

It seems that it only gradually dawned on Swedenborg that his quest for God demanded that he change internally. The early Swedenborg could only see God as a rather remote, cold intellectual theology. To truly see God the whole inwardness of Swedenborg had to be opened and intensified. He had to be instructed in the inner, subtle, rich language of feeling-image-symbolism. The whole feeling side of him had to be awakened and take a position superior to intellect. Hence, in the image above, he is the servant of the virgins, who happily give themselves just to lovers. These were the major changes in him as he went within. One minor conflict was that the inner wanted to call him away from his scientific preoccupation. At first he kept relating inner imagery to his scientific work. But he began to see that the inner carried a larger message. The inner described him as very swift (indeed, he produced scientific work at lightning speed), but at great cost. He had so much invested in the scientific effort that it took something like a year for the inner to pull him from this preoccupation. Though, for a time, he tried to use the inner processes to gain time for his scientific work, the inner hammered him out of this preconception. The real issue became his relationship to the inner and how well he understood and accepted its trends.

The changes in Emanuel Swedenborg illustrate the usual effects of the successful journey within. The former habitual standpoint of consciousness (in his case hyperintellectualism) encounters its opposite (feeling). The conscious orientation misunderstands its opposite. Swedenborg, for instance, at first thought the inner was commenting on and assisting his scientific work. As the encounter with the opposite increases there is considerable storm, fear, and vascillation on the part of the habitual consciousness. Gradually these opposite values mix (i.e., intellect becomes more feelingful and feeling becomes more rational). The encounter resolves into a new standpoint for consciousness that combines these opposite values. In Swedenborg's case this union is illustrated by the productive union of feeling and thought through all his later works. This new standpoint of consciousness is symbolized by his comments on his being a servant of the virgins. The result of the journey within is a fundamental broadening of the individual's values and perspective that takes account of what used to be habitually overlooked and discounted. Whereas he habitually saw everything in intellectual terms, the inner represented his scientific work as a load of rubbish the poor man was pulling. The new viewpoint was contained in the very feelingful symbolism he came to appreciate.

His prior religious training and experience actually served him well. He sought God above all else and believed that God could show from within, placing him in a respectful supplicant position. Forces that would terrify a nonreligious man he could meet with and accept easily. At the same time his religion was not naïve. There were other spirits within as well, and he had to sort out their quality and usefulness. He suspected his ignorance and unworthiness in relation to these inner forces. He easily accepted rather disparaging criticism from the unconscious. The sense of his unworthiness and childlike understanding deepened as he went within, until he described himself as being wet-nursed like an infant. This attitude toward his own lowliness enabled him to move faster in this realm. The *Journal of Dreams* pretty well covers his personal analysis, yet it covers only a period of seven months.

Toward the end of the *Journal* his dreams have a soaring quality. He is dealing with great forces. All bodes well.

I saw a great king; it was the King of France, who went about without a suite and in such lowly estate that he could not be recognized as a king. There was one with me who did not seem willing to acknowledge him as king, but I said that he is of such a character as to care nothing for it. He was very courteous towards all, without distinction, and spoke also with me. As he left he was still without a suite and took upon himself the burdens of others, and carried as it were a load of clothes; but later he came into a very different company, where there was much more magnificent estate. Afterwards I saw the queen; a chamberlain then came and bowed before her, and she also made just as deep a reverence, and there was nothing of pride in her. JD 274–275

The king he related directly to Christ. It is possible in this stage to become overinflated by identifying with the good forces within. Characteristically Swedenborg identified most with lowly parts of dreams. The king had to be the Christ who moved inauspiciously among men and carried their burden. An earlier dream had Swedenborg carrying rags, here it is Christ. The great feminine verity is also present as the queen, but she too acts without pride. Swedenborg himself was rapidly becoming unprideful. That the king was not fully known means that Swedenborg himself didn't know or fully recognize the Christ yet.

There followed a dream with a very intimate playfulness between Christ and Swedenborg.

It seemed as if it were Christ Himself, with whom I associated as with another person, without ceremony. He borrowed a little money from another person, about five pounds. I was vexed because he did not borrow from me. I took up two pounds, but it seemed to me that I dropped one of them, and likewise the other one. He asked what it was. I said that I had found two, and that one of them might have been dropped by Him. I handed them over, and He accepted. In such an innocent manner we seemed to live together, which was a state of innocence. JD 276

At this time Swedenborg started work on *The Worship and Love of God* (in later years he didn't seem to think much of this unusual work). It was as though he wanted to celebrate his new way of feeling and understanding. The book was very unlike anything he had ever done before. It was an epic poem, a youthful celebration. He allowed his inner feeling and imagination to burst forth in a colorful description of the creation of the universe and of man. It presaged much of what he was to find later in the Bible. He was free of the labored, tight, intellectual way in which he had always functioned in the past. Early in the writing of this book he has this short dream, which very much describes the book. "It seemed as if a sky-rocket burst above me, shedding a mass of sparks of beautiful fire. It means, perhaps, love for what is high" (JD 285).

Notice in what follows how clear feeling is and how it combines with understanding and what is elevated. The following from *The Worship and Love of God* (paragraphs 111–112) described Adam and Eve in the Garden of Eden. They are about to begin their married life. Try to visualize the scenes presented with their rich imagery.

When now she was left alone to her only one, in order that they might pass pleasantly the intermediate time until evening, for the sun was still equidistant from its rising and its setting, the bride led about her bridegroom by the hand through her natal grove and its magnificent palestra and scenes, for it was like the most pleasant theatre of the orb. They met nothing which did not fill all the senses with the pleasantness of beauty, and at the same time everything gave opportunity for conversation and turned this first experience of their lives into intimacy; from which the youth could not but turn the conversation to the testification of his love. For all things were in vernal flower and genial sport, and as it were enticed the pledges of union with the love which burned to hasten the unition of the associate mind. Everything was auspicious, heaven itself favoring; wherefore no delay interposed until the bride also burned with a like torch of mutual love and declared herself as favorable and pleased at the coming of her bridegroom, for which favor he humbly gave thanks and declared her to be his one only delight in the world, the beauty and the crown of his life which, placed upon his head by the heavenly ones, he accepted as a bond to his fidelity. Thus there was consent by both, and a covenant, which they also confirmed by mutual kisses. The love thence conceived and born grew and slowly became a flame. For in that most perfect state of their minds' life a pure innocence with delights most sweet and affecting to this new born infancy nourished and incited this love. From these auspicious beginnings a new condition of life, distinct from the former and not hitherto perceived, entered into both; namely, nothing presented to sense smiled upon and was pleasing to one which did not also affect the mind of the other; and thus from consent their gladness was united and exalted; so that the vein of all delights inflowed into a heart as it were united, but divided into two chambers. There it joined itself into a common stream (each part of) which did not sweetly taste its own pleasure without at the same time tasting also that of the other.

In the early morn, when Aurora sent forth on high into the hemisphere of heaven the rays of the rising sun, like arrows tinged with gold, they both awoke at the same time from a most sweet sleep in the conjugial couch which they had shared; for a kind of heavenly lightning glanced over their eyes, driving away rest and drawing the attention of both away from each other and to itself. There appeared something in a middle region of heaven which was to display and signify the universe with its destinies and inmost certainties; this presented itself to the sight of both as in clear daylight.

First: There shone forth a Centre of Dazzling Light, of such infinite brightness that the solar flames, radiated from Aurora, retired into shade, and the glowing torches of the constellations immediately disappeared. Thence also the eyes of both began to blink so that they were altogether compelled to close them with their lids; but nevertheless the splendor shone so clearly that it flashed through to the purest points of the fibres. This Centre so poured forth Its Light through the universe that its terminations or ends vanished from the sight, and then, because of the incomprehensibility, a blackish stupor was poured forth into the spheres of all the senses.

Secondly; Round about this Most Bright and Spacious Centre there appeared to be produced a Border, purple from brilliancy, but flamy, glittering with a transparent beauty, tinged with a Tyrian hue, a circle of gems. This was flowing about into perpetual orbits, in number like those of an endless Meander. The orbits gyrated in perennial courses and revolved their ends from firsts to lasts and when they had revolved insinuated them again in firsts. The gyres were constant, but because they entered into and receded from each other, the sight following them was led astray, although the revolutions of all flowed and reflowed most uniformly. This border and its meandering banks were crowned by most beautiful faces and forms of bodies the foreheads of which were encircled by gems like little stars, which were also surrounded by a yellow border. All the forms resembled the first-born and his most beautiful companion and represented loves like them in the beautiful couch in which they reclined.

Swedenborg's feeling and imagery burst forth, presenting symbols and symbols within symbols growing, comprehending all. The inner process predicted this book would be written and probably had a hand in it. My best guess is that the inner felt that Swedenborg badly needed to practice the expression of this inner feeling symbolism. The book was practice. Yet hidden in its rich imaginative symbolism is almost every idea he was to discover later. The book was practice in a new way of living and experiencing, practice he needed. Yet it was not based on any direct experience, so he counts it a youthful exuberant work.

Essentially Swedenborg had finished the self-analysis and inner changes he inadvertantly undertook when he went within to find the psyche, or soul. His real aim was finding God, the highest and most useful of all the verities. Inner psychic/spiritual visionary experience was now possible in almost any sphere or sense. Most of it still occurred near sleep, but he was also having photisms, or the guiding flame, in the daytime. He also seemed to have tremendously enriched imagery and presentiments of new truths at any time of day. Exploration of the hypnogogic state and the yogic meditation he used tended to change even waking consciousness.

At this point Swedenborg was a scientist who had really opened a whole new sphere. The direction he should take from now on was not clear to him. He prayed for guidance, and within a few months, the guidance came. The same spirit in which Swedenborg tried to master the world of science he carried into his psychological/spiritual explorations. The inner struck him down for this before more was shown him.

I was in London and dined rather late at the inn where I was in the habit of dining, and where I had my own room. My thoughts were engaged on the subject we have been discussing. I was hungry and ate with a good appetite. Towards the close of the meal I noticed a sort of dimness before my eyes; this became denser, and I then saw the floor covered with horrid crawling reptiles, such as snakes, frogs, and similar creatures. I was amazed; for I was perfectly conscious, and my thoughts were clear. At last the darkness increased still more; but it disappeared all at once, and I then saw a man sitting in the corner of the room; as I was then alone, I was very much frightened at his words, for he said: "Eat not so much." All became black again before my eyes, but immediately it cleared away, and I found myself alone in the room. Docs I, p. 35

Finally the visionary tendency broke into his waking life. It was frightening. He had overindulged in eating, and the message seemed to scourge him for this. But I agree with Acton that this too is probably symbolic.[15] The symbol is appropriate, for he probably felt guilty for having eaten so much. But the incident began with his thinking of the recent conversation downstairs. He was thinking from self and indulging himself too much. Darkness grew and there were crawly things all over the floor. It was like a warning. Don't eat—think—indulge yourself so much or you will make darkness and horror. He recalled this incident years later when talking to a friend. He associated this with the idea of people who thought so much that they led themselves astray. "We must not, by our own power and by own intelligence, begin to doubt the heavenly truths which are revealed to us. . . . You are well aware how often it has happened, that students and especially theologians, who unnecessarily indulged too much in speculations, have lost their understanding" (Docs I, p. 35). Hence Swedenborg, the master of all the sciences, was put down for presuming to figure out this inner world. But the vision returned.

Such an unexpected terror hastened my return home; I did not let the landlord notice anything; but I considered well what had happened, I could not look upon it as a mere matter of chance, or as if it had been produced by a physical cause.

I went home; and during the same night the same man revealed himself to me again, but I was not frightened now. He then said that he was the Lord God, the Creator of the world, and the Redeemer, and that he had chosen me to explain to men the spiritual sense of the Scripture, and that He Himself would explain to me what I should write on this subject; that same night were opened to me so that I became thoroughly convinced of their reality, the worlds of spirits, heaven, and hell, and I recognized there many acquaintances of every condition in life. From that day I gave up the study of all worldly science, and laboured in spiritual things, according as the Lord had commanded me to write. Afterwards the Lord opened, daily very often, my bodily eyes, so that, in the middle of the day I could see into the other world, and in a state of perfect wakefulness converse with angels and spirits. Docs I, pp. 35–36

In another place the man he had seen was described as "in imperial purple and in majestic light" (Docs II, p. 426).

The last obstacle to the personal changes needed in Swedenborg was removed. He could not presume by his own intelligence to deduce anything of this new realm. He would be shown; he was to be guided from within. The long effort of the inner to call him away from science was complete. He didn't even finish *The Worship and Love of God,* which he had been working on. The personal changes required in him were now complete. He had broken through the personal inner world. The rest of his work would describe what he felt was beyond. The man who was slapped down for presuming too much with his intellect turned out to be a very faithful recorder of heaven and hell and all the universes beyond man. His outer life was so sane and normal that it was many years before anyone knew that he also walked in heaven and hell.

Swedenborg took this direct commission quite seriously. He turned to master the Bible in order to show its inner meanings to the world. This meant years of quiet scholarship. There would be no more publications for a while. He perfected his biblical Hebrew and Greek, for he wanted to see the original words themselves. His style was to develop his own indexes and rely on these.

There began to come from his pen an eight-volume work, *The Word Explained,* an exposition of the inner meanings in the Bible. The scholar can find in it the beginnings of what was later to be his full understanding. Though he intended it for publication, his interest waned and it was only published after his death by his followers. This work was part of his exhaustive study of the Bible, where he found some of the same symbolism he had found in inner states. Sprinkled here and there are references to spiritual experiences. There are curious references to automatic writing (WE 459, 1150). Apparently he felt his hand seized and he wrote things of biblical figures that he didn't even approve of. He was becoming acquainted with what will be described later as lower-order spirits. The automatic writing seemed to have appeared for just a while; it disappeared when he didn't trust it as a process. He was learning in both the spiritual and biblical realms. *The Word Explained* is not really worth reading, except by scholars who want to trace his development. Its initial insights were later to be replaced by the *Arcana Coelestia,* his mature masterwork.

A year after his commission by the Lord in 1745 he began his five-volume *Spiritual Diary.* These are his running notes on experiences in the spiritual world. It was not intended for publication either and appeared posthumously, a much more valuable work than *The Word Explained.*

Early quotations will suggest the kind of experiences he was having.

During the night between October 29 and 30, 1747 I had a dream from which I awoke repeatedly; for evil spirits kept on infesting me, so much so that I could not continue to sleep. After awakening several times . . . I was seized with a trembling throughout the whole body, and I manifestly perceived that a certain column, as it were, surrounded me; I could sensibly perceive it. I awaited what would thence happen. . . . It was continually insinuated into my thought . . . that this was the "brazen wall," as it is called (Jer. i 18; xv. 20), by which the faithful are defended from the infestation of evil spirits. . . . afterwards, when I was in hell, and indeed in the body as I am today, a certain one of those miserable beings was permitted to speak to me, which he also did for some considerable time. . . . They complained of those free spirits or "furies," who as yet lodge in the third heaven, that they are the ones who torment them; for their desire is to torment every man and spirit whatsoever. In a word, their torments are unspeakable; but I was allowed to encourage them with some hope. SD 228

There was a certain soul with evil spirits around him, who, as I can surmise, never supposed otherwise than that he thought and did each and all things of himself. In order that it might appear clearly before the souls and spirits standing around how such a soul is led, and that he speaks and says nothing whatever except what inflows through the spirits who are around him, and invisible to him, there was dictated a merely trifling expression, and—as usually happens in the spiritual heaven—it appeared and was heard. This word, having been sent down, rolled about among the spirits, and thus came to all who were speaking; and the soul in the midst thus supposed that he spoke from himself, nor could he know otherwise. SD 315

Today, some of those who were in heaven were desirous of knowing what heavenly joy is. It was therefore also granted them, by the mercy of God-Messiah, to feel the heavenly joy to their inmost degree, even to such an extent that they could bear it no more. SD 314

In this way he systematically kept track of spiritual experiences for nineteen years. The *Spiritual Diary* is a jungle of visionary experiences. It is almost too raw, too rich, too full of odd discoveries, clues to the arcane, and the tangle of devious spirits. It is good that Swedenborg, the careful expositor of truth, distilled out of this a coherent picture of the worlds beyond this one. This mining engineer had come a long way.

4

Worlds Within Worlds:
Heaven and Hell

ALL ANGELS + SPIRITS WERE ONCE MEN ON EARTH.?

Swedenborg's claim that he was permitted to walk in heaven and hell was one of his most controversial claims.

I am well aware that many will say that no one can possibly speak with spirits and angels so long as he lives in the body; and many will say that it is ▓▓ a phantasy, others that I relate such things in order to gain credence, and others will make other objections. But by all this I am not deterred, for I have seen, I have heard, I have felt. AC 68

Only his experience of the highest heavens and of the lowest hells seemed limited. Yet it may have been only that these were more difficult to describe. His experiences of heaven and hell first came in trance states. Later it became easier for him to explore these areas even in the midst of ordinary daily activities. After his introduction into these regions there followed four years of exploration with no publications. The first work that came from the mature spiritual explorer was the great *Arcana Coelestia*. Some thirteen years after the opening of the spiritual worlds to him,

Heaven and Hell appeared. Though references to the nature of the worlds beyond this one are scattered through ▇ his works from the *Arcana* on, *Heaven and Hell* was a mature pulling together and summarizing of the worlds beyond. (Incidentally, ▇ his great works from the *Arcana* on were published anonymously, until close to the end of his life. His great works came from the pen of an unknown servant of the Lord.) The heavy intellectual style of his scientific works was gone. He spoke in a seasoned, balanced, unassuming, and very direct way of his amazing discoveries. There was no speculation, no doubt, no ambiguity. As well as he could, in relatively simple Latin prose, he set forth what he knew and experienced. Yet it becomes apparent that he was speaking of new dimensions of human experience. Not all sensed the essential newness and vast scope of implications of what he said.

At the beginning of *Heaven and Hell* he spoke of those who doubted or denied the existence of heaven and hell.

The man of the church at this day knows scarely anything of heaven and hell, or of his life after death, although these things are described in the Word. Indeed, many who are born within the church deny them, saying in their hearts, "Who has come from that world and told us?" Lest, therefore, such a denial, which prevails especially among those who have much worldly wisdom, should also infect and corrupt the simple in heart, and the simple in faith, it has been permitted me to associate with angels, and to talk with them as with man; and also to see what is in the heavens, and what is in the hells, and this for thirteen years; and to describe them from things seen and heard in the hope that ignorance may be enlightened, and unbelief dispelled. HH 1

To my knowledge there is nothing comparable to this account in the whole of world literature. Dante described heaven and hell, but his was a work of fiction based on legend and myth. Many religions imply something of heaven and hell. If one gathered together all the references in the Bible, the result would be a sketchy and ambiguous picture. This is also true of the other world religions. Myth and legend would produce an unclear and ambiguous picture. Swedenborg's description is fundamentally unlike all these. One cannot accuse him of simply inventing it, based on myth and religious references. His is fundamentally different, and yet in accord with the few fragmentary references in the Bible. It is the essential nature of the heaven and hell he described that is so different as to require some readjustment in our thinking about these regions. Spiritualists claim to contact the spiritual world. Even supposing that some do, it appears they are contacting only the lowest level of the worlds Swedenborg described—and this lowest level can be quite deceptive, as Swedenborg was to make clear.

Since few others, if any, have visited heaven and hell while living on earth, Swedenborg's account appears beyond confirmation. Yet there are several kinds of confirmation that tend to substantiate his claim though they fall short of a personal visit. For one, he was able to bring back information from these worlds that seems to lie beyond the bounds of what he could ordinarily know. These somewhat miraculous confirmations will be described in Chapter 7. Second, people with psychotic hallucinations describe experiences remarkably similar to Swedenborg's, to be covered in Chapter 6. The implication is that some part of madness consists of being thrust into an experience of worlds beyond this one, experiences that the disturbed individual neither wants nor can use. A third confirmation is that nothing that Swedenborg found was contrary to biblical revelation. In fact, he illuminated passages of Scripture that otherwise seem merely quaint or obscure. The final, most critical confirmation is internal. It will be seen that Swedenborg's heaven and hell echoed much of the innermost aspects of normal human experience. It was meant to. We are the image of all that is. This is really the most substantial, existential, and immediate of the confirmations. Should there be no heaven or hell whatsoever, Swedenborg's account would remain a most valuable and sensitive picture of the internal state of man. These confirmations will become clearer as we progress.

In a way Emanuel Swedenborg's breakthrough to heaven and hell was not a complete surprise. He had had the experience of the presence of spirits for some years. Earlier we demonstrated that any person can have the experience of faint voices in the hypnogogic state, and while many have had this experience, few have made the effort to remember or record it. Even though Swedenborg lived in an age that gave more credence to spirits than the present, he was slow to come to this explanation. After numerous dreams, visions, temptations, double thoughts, and other strange experiences, he makes one reference late in the *Journal of Dreams* (247) that he thinks a lot of these experiences can be accounted for by the presence of spirits. This would mean that the strange, symbolic words heard in the hypnogogic state actually reflect the presence of spirits. This does not deny their also being autosymbolic representations of inner states. After thirteen years of journeying in the worlds beyond this one, he finally pulled together his findings in *Heaven and Hell,* one of his greatest and most popular works. Before exploring this work, I would like to describe briefly Swedenborg's style of writing.

The Mood of Understanding

The main content of Swedenborg's theological writings is not immediately apparent. He was always speaking of inner states of man. If one is not prepared to understand inner states, his writings can easily seem abstract, dull, and pedantic.

Swedenborg wrote in Latin two centuries ago. He tended to use long sentences, cramming as much as he could into each one. They are too rich to be read hastily and need to be broken down into pieces. If you are to grasp the reach of his sentences, you may have to pause clause by clause, sentence by sentence, to get the sweep of his meaning. Swedenborg's translators have been his followers and tended to keep close to his style, creating heavy sentences in translation, only in a few instances taking the liberty to lighten up his sentence structure. Swedenborg's writings are weighted with meaning, and need to be taken by pieces, slowly. An example: "Love dwells in its affections like a lord in his domain and a king in his realm; its domain or realm is over the things of the mind, that is, of the will and understanding and thence of the body" (DP 106). This one sentence covers the whole sequence of events from the inmost love, to its affections or feelings, to the will and understanding, to control over the body. The reach of ideas is rather great for one sentence. He used the symbolism of his time (lord, king, domain). He was saying that inmost love is the force that conditions all aspects of mind and actions—an example of Swedenborg speaking of inner states. The reader gradually becomes familiar with his concepts. Elsewhere he said that what love leads into is affection (AC 3938), or the whole affective and emotional basis of mind. What an individual loves is then the root and source of all other aspects of mind and action.

Not only was Swedenborg almost always dealing with inner states, he was also always speaking existentially. The "love that dwells in its affections" sounds like an abstract idea, but it isn't. He was speaking of his own experience and asked that the reader confirm it in his own experience. At no point did Swedenborg ask that the reader take anything on faith. Elsewhere he explored the question of how thoroughly these things can be checked. He disparaged memory, or intellectual knowledge. The real is what a man does.

If anyone's memory and understanding is such that he can learn and comprehend all the truths of heaven and the church, yet has no desire to do any of them, do not people say of him, he is an intelligent man, but he is so wicked? Indeed, do they not add, he is all the more deserving of punishment? This shows that anyone who separates the spiritual from what is moral and civil, is not a spiritual man, or a moral man, nor a civil man. From experience: there are such people in the world; I have talked with some after their decease, and found that they knew everything in The Word, and accordingly knew many truths, and believed that on this account they would shine in heaven as the stars; however, when their life was examined, it was found to be merely corporeal and worldly . . . and each one became his own Will, and they were driven into hell. DLDW 149

The first truths with a man called faith, are not yet living, for they are things of memory only and, from the memory, of thinking and speaking, adjoined to his natural love which, from its desire to know, imbibes them readily, and, from its desire to boast itself on account of its knowledge or its erudition, summons them from the memory . . . to give utterance to them. These truths are first made living . . . by a life in conformity with them. DLDW 152

Even though Swedenborg was always dealing with inner states, these only became true or real when they reflect in action. What at first seems abstract is very existential, real, actual. Because of this concreteness it can and should be checked by the experience of others. Committing it to memory isn't enough. If the reader thinks of Swedenborg as always dealing with real, confirmable human experience it will sweep away the obscuring clouds of the abstract. It only looks abstract. He was always talking of existence—his and yours—since all human existence is essentially the same.[16]

Unless you are interested in inner states and ultimate knowledge, Swedenborg's writings will not attract you. We can only perceive, understand, and empathize with what echoes within ourselves. His writings are full of feeling; he repeatedly speaks of good and love, essentially feelingful concepts.

Finally the reader will discover that Swedenborg was trying to describe all that can be described. Only in speaking of some aspects of God or of the highest angels would he break off and say it is ineffable, more than can be said. Until then he described all there was: the inner and outer of man, this world, the worlds beyond this one, even other creatures on other planets. He wanted to understand it all, and he came close to that goal. Also, the reader should recognize Swedenborg's tendency to deal with psychological and spiritual matters as a single realm. It is our past teachings that have separated these. Man's mind or experience is his participation in the spiritual. These two are always dealing with life, human existence. The spiritual is the inner and ultimate aspect of the psychological. To enter the spiritual world, or be in the spirit, one needs to go inward into the roots of human experience. Because the innermost is the spiritual realm, it is possible to enter the spiritual realm through inner exploration. We won't laboriously label what is psychological or spiritual in his works since these are one realm—life itself.

With these preliminary understandings, we can summarize Swedenborg's findings on his great psychological/spiritual journey.

The Nature of Heaven

Swedenborg's description of the multiplicity of worlds or levels of being represented by the concepts of heaven and hell is so fundamentally different from legend and myth that it takes some readjustment of thinking to understand his findings. *Fundamentally, a man's life in these other worlds is based on what he really is.* In the present world a person explores, develops, and forms himself. We are quite capable of deceiving ourselves and others. In the worlds beyond this one people are sorted out according to what they really are. *They move toward the essential reality of their existence.* Thus

the worlds beyond this one are even more essentially psychological and spiritual than this one.

Swedenborg's pervasive emphasis on the most essential
nature of a person gives his whole description of other worlds
a surprising quality. In almost every aspect of his description
he moves away from petty externals and deals with essentials. He is dealing with the quality of the innermost heaven
at the same time he is dealing with the innermost quality of
mind. The reader is jarred into thinking of the real quality
of his life. The account begins to seem credible from this
aspect alone, so that the reader has to stretch his concep-
tions, and deal with the essential nature of his life, even to
begin to understand the worlds beyond this one.

Swedenborg's account begins with the issue of what a man
really is. The two essential functions of a man are understanding and willing. These psychological functions are the
operations of his soul, or spirit, or life, for the spirit is the
life. Man is a life or spirit acting within a body, a necessary
instrument so the spirit can come to earth and act in the
natural world.

Every one who weighs the subject aright may know that the
body does not think, because it is material, but the soul, because
it is spiritual. The soul of man . . . is his spirit, for this is altogether
immortal. It is the spirit which thinks in the body, for it is spiritual,
and the spiritual receives what is spiritual, and lives spiritually,
which is to think and to will. . . . [The body of man] is adjoined
to the spirit, in order that the spirit of man may live and perform
uses in the natural world. . . .

Since every thing which lives in the body, and from life acts and
feels, is solely of the spirit, and not of the body, it follows that the
spirit is the real man . . . for whatever lives and feels in man is of
his spirit, and everything in man, from the head to the sole of his
foot, lives and feels. Hence it is that when the body is separated
from its spirit, which is called dying, the man still remains, and
lives. HH 432–433

That man is a spirit as to his interiors, may be evident from this, that after the body is separated, which takes place when he dies, the man still lives as before. That I might be confirmed in this, I have been permitted to speak with almost all whom I had ever known in the life of the body; with some for hours, with others for weeks and months, and with others for years, and this principally in order that I might have proof, and that I might testify it. HH 437

When we say that man is a spirit as to his interiors, we mean, as to those things which are of his thought and will, for these are the interiors themselves, which cause man to be man, and as his interiors are, such is the man. HH 444

Swedenborg had finally found the soul. His anatomical work was unnecessary. The soul is the life, the spirit, the inner of man's experience. The quality of this life is the quality of the man. Swedenborg rejected airy, abstract ideas of the soul that are not experienced.

[After death] it is believed that he will then be a soul, and the common idea of a soul is that it consists of something like ether or air; thus that it is a breath, such as a man breathes out when he dies. It is believed, however, that this retains the essential elements of his life, but is devoid of sight like that of the eye, hearing like that of the ear, and speech like that of the mouth. Yet the fact is that after death a man is none the less a man; and so fully is he a man that he does not know but that he is still living in the former world. He sees, hears and speaks; he walks, runs and sits; he lies down, sleeps and wakes; he eats and drinks; he enjoys the delights of married life, as he did in the former world; in a word, he is in all respects a man. Thus it is evident that death is not an extinction but a continuation of life, and merely a transition from one state to another. TCR 792

Angels guided Swedenborg through the experience of dying several times so he could know what it is like. The separation from the body comes soon after the breathing and the heartbeat stop. The person gradually awakens in the inner spiritual world. He has arrived at the threshold of the other worlds. Because the person still feels and senses things and awakens in a world much like what he is accustomed to, he may at first feel he hasn't died. The first state of man after death is the state of exteriors. Everything is the same, people are the same, and he lives as before.

The first state of man after death is like his state in the world, because he is still in like manner in externals. He has therefore a similar face, a similar speech, and a similar disposition . . . so that he knows no other than that he is still in the world, unless he pays attention to the things that he meets with, and to what was said by the angels when he was raised up—that he is now a spirit. HH 493

The closest analogy would be to the world of dreams. It too seems like the plain, ordinary, real world until one looks closer and pays attention to the differences. Like dreams, he is now in a world of representations. That is, he is beginning to meet his own nature in the things, people, setting that surrounds him. This gradually becomes more apparent.

Very commonly a husband and wife come together and congratulate each other, and also continue together for a time, longer or shorter according to their delight in living together in the world. If true marriage love . . . has not joined them together, they are separated after a while. But if the minds of the partners were discordant, and were inwardly averse to each other, they burst forth into open enmity, and some times into actual fighting. HH 494

This beginning level certainly has a familiar ring to it. They are instructed regarding the spiritual world, and, of course, most conclude they will go to heaven! This is a threshold world that Swedenborg called the world of spirits. It is essentially a place where the spirit of a person is opened to its real nature. It becomes no longer possible to act one way and be another. The person pauses at this threshold world long enough to become one with his real nature. This is the judgment. The person begins to discover and drift toward his real nature.

They are therefore instructed by friends concerning the state of eternal life, and also conducted to various places, and into various companies, and sometimes into cities, gardens and paradises, and frequently to magnificent things, because such things delight the externals, in which they are. They are also by turns led into thoughts which they had in the life of the body, . . . about heaven and hell. . . . Almost all of them desire to know whether they shall come into heaven, and many believe that they shall, because they led a moral and civil life in the world, not reflecting that both the wicked and the good lead a similar life outwardly, doing good to others in the same manner, going to churches, hearing sermons, and praying; and not knowing at all that outward deeds and outward acts of worship are of no avail, but the internal states from which the external acts proceed. HH 495

Swedenborg wasn't trying to scare the reader, he was just reporting, and that is what makes it more frightening and convincing. The possibility of cheating one's way into heaven dims when the internals are opened up in the second state of the world of spirits. This is the way the eternal judgment comes.

Man, now a spirit, is let into the state of his interiors, or into the state of the interior will and its thought, in which he had been in the world when left to himself to think freely and without restraint. He falls into this state without being aware of it, just as in the world, when he withdraws the thought which is nearest to speech, or from which he speaks, towards his interior thought, and abides in that. When therefore, the man, now a spirit is in this state, he is in himself, and in his very life; for to think freely from his own affection is the very life of man, and is himself. HH 502

When a spirit is in the state of his interiors, it manifestly appears of what quality the man was in himself when in the world. . . . He who was interiorly good in the world, now acts rationally and wisely, and indeed more wisely than in the world, because he is released from connection with the body, and therefore from earthly things, which caused obscurity and interposed, as it were, a cloud. But he who was in evil in the world, now acts foolishly and insanely, more insanely, indeed than in the world, because he is in freedom, and unrestrained. When he lived in the world, he was sane, in outward appearance, for he thereby feigned himself a rational man; but when the outward appearance is taken away from him, his insanities are revealed. A bad man, who outwardly takes the semblance of good, may be compared to a covered vessel, bright and polished on the outside, and covered with a lid, in which is concealed filth of all kinds; according to the Lord's declaration, "Ye are like unto whited sepulchers, which outwardly appear beautiful, but within are full of dead man's bones, and of all uncleanness" (Matt. xxiii, 27). HH 505

A person can even go through the opening of the Book of Lives in which every detail of the life is reviewed (HH 463). Occasionally, Swedenborg said something that sounded strange until you look at its psychological validity. "When a man's acts are discovered to him after death, the angels, whose duty it is to make the search, look into his face, and extend their examination through the entire body, beginning with the fingers of each hand, and thus proceeding through the whole" (HH 463).

Swedenborg was himself surprised at this procedure. It had to be explained. Everything a person has done is written in the nervous system. The fingertips represent actual deeds. Hence the examination is begun there and works toward the interiors. This is another aspect of a person discovering what he actually is. The opening of the Book of Lives is a detailed review of everything you have been and done.

The next state after death is one in which a man is instructed. He has discovered what he really is, what his real tendencies are, a somewhat humbling experience. Those who are self-selecting themselves for heaven wish to know more of the worlds beyond this one. This need is met by angelic instruction. Others, when opened, have fallen into their own grossness. They appear less wise than they did in the world —much like the impressive fellow who shows that he is a fool when drunk. These people close themselves to instruction. They don't sense the vast spiritual worlds beyond this one. They fall into their inner tendencies and drift toward the hell that matches them.

The distinction between the heavens and the hells is a critical one that Swedenborg described in many ways. The attitude that causes a drift toward heaven is in the feeling that there is a higher power and an effort to relate to it. This same spirit of humility and respect for the greatness of creation goes with an effort to be with others and to be of some use. By this a person faces toward heaven. The nature of heaven reflects in Swedenborg's statement that in heaven the joy of one is the joy of all. The opposite attitude is to put down creation and elevate the self. The one bound for hell serves himself first, last, and foremost. By this he is cut off from the opening-out possibilities of heaven and becomes enclosed in concerns for himself over and above others. The distinction between heaven and hell will become clearer, but this is the fundamental difference. Heaven must be a very shared place. Hell is a very cut-off place where each strugles against others. Of course, in this world we all experience both tendencies. How much each individual has adopted a heaven-like or hell-like approach becomes more manifest as the essentials of his life are opened. Even in the instruction of those who have selected themselves for heaven the emphasis is on the life, not on memory learning, as is most common in this world. The following is one of Swedenborg's many beautiful passages in which he had a feeling for this essential quality of heaven. It is a little too rich to grasp all at once.

Instructions in the heavens differ from instructions on earth in this respect, that knowledges are not committed to memory, but to life; for the memory of spirits is in their life, because they receive and imbibe everything which agrees with their life, and do not receive, much less imbibe, anything which does not agree with it; for spirits are affections and therefore in a human form similar to their affections. HH 517

The knowledge of spirits is in what they do. This is a more existential or fundamental conception of knowledge than we are accustomed to. Because it is of the life, they only learn what they can act on. What their disposition does not permit them to live out, they do not learn. Essentially, spirits are affections or feelings, the inner or essential aspects of mind that underly mere thought or memory. When stripped of the body and the less essential aspects of mind, these affections are even more in the form of a man. Or—another way of saying it—the essential of a person is even more a person. "This being the case with them, the affection for truth is continually inspired for the sake of the uses of life; for the Lord provides that everyone should love the uses suited to his peculiar disposition" (HH 517).

Use was a fundamental idea with Swedenborg. He said elsewhere that heaven is a kingdom of uses. Everyone there does something to contribute to the general good. This is part of its shared quality and its happiness. Each follows the uses that reflect his basic disposition. He is then bent for heaven, as all are who live out their uses. The shared quality of heaven becomes more apparent in the next lines.

And since all the uses of heaven have reference to the common use, which is for the Lord's kingdom, for that kingdom is their country, and since all particular and individual uses are excellent in proportion as they relate more nearly and more fully to the common use, therefore all particular and individual uses, which are innumerable, are good and heavenly. Therefore, with every one, the affection for truth is conjoined so intimately with the affection for use, that they make one; by this means, truth is implanted in use, so that the truths which they learn are truths of use. In this manner angelic spirits are instructed, and prepared for heaven. The affection for truth which regards use is insinuated by various means, most of which are unknown in the world; chiefly by representatives of uses which in the spiritual world are presented in a thousand ways, and with such delights and pleasures that they penetrate the spirit from the interiors of his mind to the exteriors of his body, and thus effect the whole. Hence the spirit becomes, as it were, his own use; and therefore when he enters his own society, into which he is initiated by instruction, he is in his own use. From these things it may be evident, that knowledges, which are external truths, do not introduce any one to heaven, but life itself, which is a life of use. HH 517

And so the person, having become his most essential self and use, joins a society in heaven. He joins the multitude of others, friends, who are in essentially the same use.

There are three levels of heaven beyond this intermediate world of spirits: the natural heaven, the spiritual heaven, and the celestial heaven. All the spirits in these heavens or kingdoms were once persons in the world. In many respects the life of heaven cannot be understood as a simple extension of life in the world. Much of the character of the spiritual world is more nearly an extension of our inner experience. For instance, there is no time or space in heaven as we know it. In fact, Swedenborg said that ideas of time and space could impede our understanding of heaven. What corresponds to time is change of state. This is very like psychological time, which is more an inner state. It is much freer than the inexorable clock time of our world. A pleasant state seems short, an unpleasant one long. The endlessly frustrating dream may have taken a few minutes. A peaceful night's sleep can seem like a minute or two. The time of heaven is the *always now* time of the inner state.

I was thinking about eternity, and by the idea of time I could perceive what eternity might be, namely existence without end, but

not what from eternity is, and so not what God had done from
eternity before creation. When anxiety on this account arose in my
mind, I was elevated into the sphere of heaven and thus into that
perception of eternity in which angels are, and then it was made
clear to me that we must ▓▓ think of eternity from time, but from
state; and then we may perceive what ▓▓▓ eternity is, as then
happened to me. HH 167

He then had an ecstatic experience of the whole of creation.

The natural man may suppose that he would have no thought, if
the ideas of time, space and material things, were taken away, for
upon these ideas is founded ▓▓ men's thought. But let him know,
that ▓▓ thoughts are limited and confined so far as they partake
of time, space, and matter; and that they are unlimited and extended, so far as they do not partake of them. . . . Hence the angels
have wisdom, and ▓▓▓ wisdom is called incomprehensible, because it does not fall into ▓▓▓ ideas. HH 169

Similarly there is no space in heaven. What corresponds
to distance is the feelings people have for each other. We also
know the experience of being close to some and distant from
others, regardless of the actual distances involved.

They are near to each other who are in similar states, and distant,
who are in dissimilar states; and that spaces in heaven are merely
external states corresponding to internal. From this cause alone the
heavens are distinct from one another, and also the societies of each
heaven, and the individuals in each society. This is also the reason
why the hells are ▓▓▓▓▓ separated from the heavens, for they are
in a contrary state.

From the same cause also, in the spiritual world, one person
becomes present to another provided only he intensely desires his
presence, for thus he sees him in thought, and puts himself in his
state; and conversely, one person is removed from another so far
as he is averse to him. . . .

When also anyone goes from one place to another, whether it is
in his own city, or in the courts, or the gardens, or to others out
of his own society, he arrives sooner when he eagerly desires it, and
later when he does not, the way itself being lengthened or short-

ened according to the desire, although it is the same way. . . . This may be illustrated by the thoughts of man . . . for what a man views intently in thought, becomes as it were present to him. HH 193–196

This inner quality of psychological space/time becomes even more psychological when Swedenborg reports on how the external settings of angels are arranged. What the spirit experiences is a reflection of inner experiences. Things in the spiritual world can only be seen by spiritual sight. What is seen and experienced is representative of the inner states. Spiritually rich inner states reflect in a surrounding that is gorgeous and rich. Barren inner states reflect in barren surroundings. The spirit experiences what it is. On earth this is called projection. Our pervasive tendency to see and experience essentially what reflects ourselves is used in psychological projective tests. Asked to describe what is seen in an amorphous inkblot, people describe things that accurately reflect their inner nature.[17] Apparently this little appreciated phenomena is even more accentuated in heaven. Yet it is already our real tendency to notice and experience in the world what reflects us inwardly. The thief experiences a world in which everyone takes what he can get. In the same setting the artist experiences the beauty of the things around him. What we encounter in the world reflects our nature.

In all respects heaven resembles life on earth except that it is more in its essentials. Corresponding to governments on earth there is government in heaven. But those are given power who are of use to others. There are buildings, cities, hills, woods, etc., but these are psychological realities corresponding to inner states. There are meals, but spiritual food has inner implications for the life and development of individuals. The garments one finds in the closet reflect changes in one's qualities. Everyone lives in societies of people with similar uses and disposition much as we might see in the Italian or Chinese section of a large city. But there is a universal language of understanding in heaven.

The speech of spirits with one another is not a speech of words, but of ideas, such as are those of human thought without words, on which account it is the universal of all languages. But when they speak with a man, their speech falls into the words of the man's language. When I have spoken with spirits about this, it has been granted me to say that when they are conversing with one another, they cannot utter even one single word of human language, still less any name. AC 1876

Some tried to utter our words but found the process of expelling air too grossly material.

Everyone has work to do. Heaven is not a place of idleness.

Certain spirits from an opinion conceived in the world, believed heavenly happiness to consist in an idle life in which they would be served by others . . . since everyone would wish for it, none would have it. Such a life would not be active but idle, in which the faculties would become torpid; when yet it may be known to them that without activity there can be no happiness. . . . It was afterward shown by many evidences, that angelic life consists in performing the goods of charity, which are uses. . . . They who had the idea that heavenly joy consists in a life of indolence, and in breathing eternal joy in idleness, were allowed some experience of such a life . . . and they perceived it was most sad. HH 403

Swedenborg described only some of the work performed in heaven. Each society has a particular function. Some are involved in religious affairs, others in civil government; still others instruct children and infants.

These employments of angels are their general employments, but everyone has his own particular duty, for every general use is composed of innumerable ones, which are called mediate, ministering and subservient uses. All and each are coordinated and subordinated according to Divine order, and taken together, make and perfect the general use, which is the common good. HH 392

[A]ngels testified, that in the performance of such good works there is the fullest freedom, because it proceeds from interior affection, and is conjoined with ineffable delight. HH 404

How great—the delight of heaven is, may appear from this circumstance alone, that it is delightful to all in heaven to communicate their delights and blessings to others; and since all in heaven are of this character, it is plain how immense is the delight of heaven; for . . . in the heavens there is a communication of all with each and of each with all. HH 399

It takes little imagination to see how such a social organization would be heavenly. Swedenborg described the delights of heaven.

In order that I might know the nature and quality of heaven and heavenly joy, it has been granted me by the Lord frequently, and for a long time together, to perceive the delights of heavenly joys. Therefore, I know them from living experience, but can never describe them; a few observations, however, may convey some idea of them. Heavenly joy is an affection of innumerable delights and joys, which, taken together, present something general, and in these general things or general affections there are harmonies of innumerable affections . . . things innumerable are in it in such order as can never be described, those innumerable things being such as flow from the order of heaven. . . . In a word, infinite things arranged in most perfect order are in every general affection; and not one of them but lives, and affects the rest from the inmosts, for from inmosts heavenly joys proceed. HH 413

The immensity of heaven is beyond description for it includes not only all who have lived on earth but all those from other planets in the universe as well. Swedenborg affirmed that he had met others from other planets and that there were innumerable inhabited planets in the universe. He underlined the diversity of people that made up heaven. In several places he indicated that endless diversity of people is part of the beauty of heaven.

... when a one is composed of various parts, and the various parts are in a perfect form, in which each part adjoins itself to the rest in a series of harmonious agreement, then it is perfect. Now heaven is a one composed of various parts arranged in the most perfect form; for the heavenly form is the most perfect of all forms. HH 56

The highest or innermost of the three heavens is the celestial kingdom. It is distinctly and qualitatively different from the spiritual heaven. The language used is richer and more ineffable. The light is more intense. It is more interior, a world of affections or feelings. It is the will part of the heavens, while the spiritual kingdom is the understanding part. The people there are radiant. The highest of them experience themselves as the will of God. The love that binds them together is the love of God, whereas the common love in the spiritual heaven is love of the neighbor. The angels there are in great innocence and wisdom. Life and energy flow from the Lord into the celestial heaven, then into the lower spiritual heaven, and from there into the outermost heaven. Perfection increases inwardly in all things.

The angels in the Lord's celestial kingdom far excel in wisdom and glory the angels who are in His spiritual kingdom, because they receive the Divine of the Lord more interiorly; for they are in love to Him, and are therefore nearer and more closely conjoined to Him. They ... receive Divine truths immediately into the life, and not, like the spiritual, first in memory and thought; thus they have them written in their hearts ... nor do they ever reason concerning them whether the truth is so or not. ... Such angels know at once, by influx from the Lord, whether the truth which they hear is truth; for the Lord flows in. HH 25–26

There are some who came from the world and soon find their place in the celestial heaven. Others gradually progress there.

It is worthy of mention, being wholly unknown in the world, that the states of good spirits and of angels are continually changing and perfecting, and that they are thus conveyed into the interiors of the province in which they are, and so into nobler functions. For in heaven there is a continual purification, and, so to speak, a new creation; but still the case is such that no angel can possibly attain absolute perfection even to eternity. The Lord alone is perfect. AC 4803

It is clear that the progression from the world of spirits to the lowest heaven, to the spiritual heaven, to the celestial heaven forms a graduated series of spiritual perfections. Beyond that there is the Lord, who is the inmost and highest. All in heaven see and know the Lord in the light in which they are. It could not be otherwise. It is, of course, true here too.

Hell

The tendencies of hell are the opposite of those in heaven. This alone causes a fundamental separation of these kingdoms. The general design of heaven drifts toward joining with, working with, and loving others, which drifts toward the fundamental of the Divine. The general design of hell is an orientation toward self over others. This splits existence apart and causes dissension. We've all experienced both of these tendencies in ourselves, so we have a foretaste of future worlds.

If a person's real orientation is toward self over others, he will most comfortably drift toward the company of like persons in hell. In effect, we are judged by what we have made of ourselves. There are several aspects of this primary orientation for oneself. It may imply an emphasis on personal comfort, sensory experience, or wealth at the expense of others. It may imply a need to gain control over others. It is often reflected in an irritation over religious matters, or worse yet, an opposition to the Divine. In all these aspects this orientation tends to tear them apart from others and apart from the wonder of creation. Swedenborg casually mentioned even bishops he had met in hell.

It may not be apparent at first sight why hell exists or is a necessary reflection of divine love. The Lord might have designed creation so that everything was good. We would still distinguish degrees of good and came back toward the polar opposites of good and evil. Opposites, degrees of difference, are necessary for there to be understanding. Hell, as an opposite of heaven, is part of this clarification of creation. Furthermore, it is part of the range of differences that increase the wonder of creation. Just as different languages, cultures, styles, ages, circumstances, and faces enrich this world, hell is part of the enrichment of ultimate possibilities.

But larger than this is the issue of man's freedom. One could really question the amount of freedom of choice involved if everyone ended up in heaven. For Swedenborg, God loved man enough to give him the real freedom to live well or ill. Further, he said that only choices really made in freedom count. For this reason he played down the real miracles he was able to perform. Miracles coerce belief. He would rather leave belief free to choose. Heaven and hell are the cosmic polarity of differences that reflect the real gift of choice. Man designs and eventually comes to the world of his own choices. Those who go to hell feel better there. It suits them better than heaven. The opposition and equilibrium of heaven and hell is a cosmic, ultimate representation of diversity and freedom.

. . . the relation of heaven to hell . . . is like that of two opposites, which act contrary to each other, from whose action and re-action results equilibrium in which all things subsist. . . . [I t] is a spiritual equilibrium, namely of falsity against truth, and of evil against good. From hell falsity from evil is continually breathed forth, and from heaven that which is true from good. This spiritual equilibrium keeps man in freedom of thinking and willing, for whatever a man thinks and wills has relation either to evil and its falsity, or to good and its truth. Consequently when he is in that equilibrium he is free. HH 537

This equilibrium of opposites has to do even with our possibilities of perception. We must have darkness in order to appreciate light. This is true both in a natural and in a spiritual sense.

Hell is divided into societies in the same manner as heaven, and also into as many societies as heaven; for every society in heaven has a society opposite to it in hell, and this for the sake of equilibrium. But the societies in hell are distinct according to evils and their falsities, because the societies in heaven are distinct according to goods and their truth. That every good has an opposite evil, and every truth an opposite falsity, may be known from this, that there is not anything that has not reference to its opposite, and that its quality and degree is known from its opposite and its degree; and this is the origin of all perception and sensation. On this account the Lord continually provides, that every society of heaven has its opposite in a society of hell, and that there is equilibrium between them. HH 541

As in many other instances, Swedenborg was also speaking of the interior life of man as a reflection or image of the giant cosmic opposites of heaven and hell. He was always in the midst of palpable existence:

They who are in a state of enlightenment, see further, that good and evil are opposites; that they are opposite in the same way as heaven and hell are, that good is from heaven, and evil from hell; since the Divine of the Lord makes heaven—nothing flows in with man from the Lord but good, nor anything but evil from hell; and thus the Lord is continually withdrawing man from evil, and leading him to good, while hell is continually leading man into evil. Unless man were between both, he would not have any thought, nor any will, and still less any freedom and any choice; for man has all these by virtue of the equilibrium between good and evil. From these things it is plain, that the Lord flows into every man with good, the evil and good alike, but that the difference is in man himself, because he is a recipient. HH 546

Man is a recipient of both good and evil; and has a choice. The lifetime of choices determines his fate here and in the world beyond. The evil man receives good and converts it into evil, internally.

man's will and love remains with him after death. He who wills and loves evil in the world, wills and loves the same evil in the other life, and then he no longer suffers to be withdrawn, . This is the reason that a man who is in evil is bound to hell, and is actually there as to his spirit; after death desires nothing more than to be where his evil is; consequently man after death casts himself into hell, not the Lord. HH 547

Evils and falsities are like black clouds interposed between the sun and the eye, which take away serenity of light, though the sun remains in endeavor to dissipate the opposing clouds, it is shining behind them, and meanwhile transmits something of shady light into the eye of man by various roundabout ways. It is the same in the spiritual world. HH 549

Evil will strike some as a out worn idea that stirs up images of the devil and dull sermons. Swedenborg said elsewhere, "Evil viewed in itself, and sin, is nothing but disjunction from good; evil itself consists in disunion" (AC 4997). Hell is made up of those who disunite from others. The spirit of heaven is to do to others as we would have them do to us. Later we will see a mystical implication of this in that we are one To set one as better than another tears existence. This tearing apart of of existence, called evil, carries with it punishment. "Evil is so joined with punishment that they cannot be separated" (HH 550). The one who splits himself apart from others enjoys them less. This is quite unlike heaven, where the joy of one is the joy of all. The more opposed a person is to others, the more he finds them opposed to him. Evil or disunity fashions its ███ punishment. To persons living in this disunity the good of heaven is like a sun behind the clouds. The falsity Swedenborg speaks of as associated with evil essentially means experiencing a fragmented world and missing ███ unity of existence. All this is permitted that man may know real freedom, ███ that existence may know its full range of possibilities.

Swedenborg's description of hell isn't very nice. He said that ███ there see themselves as persons among persons, grouped in societies enjoying similar ways. It is in the light or truth of heaven that the grim truth of hell becomes apparent.

All spirits in the hells, when seen in any degree of heavenly light, appear in the ███ of ███ evil; for every one is an image of his evil, since with everyone the interiors and exteriors make one, and the interiors are visibly exhibited in the exteriors, which are the face, ███ body, ███ speech and ███ gestures. Their quality is therefore known at sight. In general, they are forms of contempt of others; of menaces against those who do not pay them respect; they are ███ of hatreds of various kinds, also of various kinds of revenge. Ferocity and cruelty from their interiors show themselves through these ███, but when others commend, venerate, and worship them, their faces are composed and have an appearance of gladness arising from delight. It is impossible to give a brief description of ███ these forms, as they really appear, for one is not like another: only between those who are in similar evil and therefore in a similar infernal society, there is a general likeness. . . . In general their faces are dreadful and void of life; like those of corpses; but in some instances they are black, and in others fiery like little torches: in others they are disfigured with pimples, warts, and large ulcers; with some no face appears, but in its stead something hairy or bony; and with some teeth only are seen. Their bodies ███ are monstrous, and ███ speech is as the speech of anger, or hatred, or of revenge for everyone speaks from ██ falsity and his tone is from ██ evil: in a word, they are ██ images of their own hell. . . . [In each society] the fierce passions of those who dwell there, are also represented by dreadful and atrocious things, which I forbear to describe. It is to be known, however, that such is the appearance of infernal spirits in the light of heaven, but among themselves they appear like men; and this is of the Lord's mercy that they may not seem as loathesome to one another as they appear before ██ angels. ██ that appearance is a fallacy, for as soon as a ray of light from heaven is let in, their human forms are turned into monstrous forms, such as they are in themselves . . . because everything appears in the light of heaven as it really is. This is why they shun the light of heaven, and cast themselves down into their ██ light, which is like that of burning charcoal, and in some cases like that of burning sulfur. This light is turned into ██ darkness, when a ray of light from heaven flows in upon it. Hence it is that the hells are said to be in thick darkness and in shade; and ██ thick darkness and shade signify falsities derived from evil ██ as ██ in hell. HH 553

The introduction to hell seems friendly enough, at first!

When, therefore, a spirit of his own accord, or from his own freedom, directs his course to hell, and enters it, he is received at first in a friendly manner, so that he believes that he has come among friends; but this only continues for a little while, during which he is explored as to his astuteness and ability. [After this] they begin to infest him by various means, and with increasing severity and vehemence. This is done by introduction more interiorly and ██ deeply into hell; for the more interior and deeper the hell, the more malignant are the spirits. After infestations they afflict him with cruel punishments, until he is reduced to a state of slavery. ██ as rebellious commotions are of continual occurrence there, because everyone desires to be the greatest, and burns with hatred against others, new insurrections are made, thus one scene is changed into another, and they who were made slaves, are delivered, that they may assist some new devil to subjugate ██; then they who do not submit themselves and obey at the word, are again tormented in various ways; and so continually. Such torments are the torments of hell, which are called hell fire. HH 574

Some of the hells have a familiar ring to them:

In the milder hells are seen, as it were, rude huts, in some cases contiguous like a city with lanes and streets. Within the houses infernal spirits are engaged in continual quarrels, enmities, blows, and fightings; in the streets and lanes, robberies and depredations are committed. In some of the hells there are mere brothels, disgusting to the sight and filled with all kinds of filth and excrement. There are also thick forests in which infernal spirits wander like wild beasts, and where too there are underground dens into which those flee who are pursued by others: deserts where all is sterile and sandy, and in some places rugged rocks containing caverns. . . . Spirits who have suffered the extremity of punishment, are cast out from the hells into these desert places, especially those who when in the world had been more cunning than others in planning and contriving artifices and deceit; their last state is such a life. HH 586

The immense multitude of people that make up heaven and hell does not exist in time and space, or—the same thing —in the material world. Theirs is a complex hierarchy of spiritual worlds visible only to the inner or spiritual sight. Even within these worlds not all can see or experience each other.

The heavens are in the higher parts of the spiritual world; in the lower parts is the world of spirits, and under all are the hells. The heavens are not visible to the spirits who are in the world of spirits, except when their interior sight is opened, although they are sometimes seen as mists or bright clouds. The reason is that the angels of heaven are in an interior state of intelligence and wisdom, and thus above the sight of those who are in the world of spirits. But spirits in the plains and valleys see one another; and yet when they are thus separated, by being let into their interiors, evil spirits do not see the good. Good spirits can see the evil, but they turn themselves away from them and spirits who turn themselves away become invisible. . . . All the gates to the hells open from the world of spirits, and none from heaven. HH 583

There is no one devil or satan. There is only the evil of evil persons.

The Principle That Unites All the Worlds

When Swedenborg started his journey inward he watched inner processes spontaneously represent themselves in images, or in things said. This was a natural example of a principle that he had suspected united all levels of existence. The inner can represent itself by images, which are of a lower order and a different nature from the inner. Dreams correspond to the person's life situation at the time they are dreamt.

The levels of existence correspond to each other, and the idea of correspondence knits all levels of existence into a related whole. The ramifications of Swedenborg's treatment of correspondence could fill several volumes in itself, but it is enough for the reader to get a general grasp of what is involved.

A great deal of our own existence involves correspondence, because the scope of our individual world works across several levels of existence. Feeling, or affection, is the most inward and fundamental aspect of mind. To this corresponds thought. In the hypnogogic state it is possible to watch feelings shape their corresponding thoughts.[18] Unless a person is trying to deceive, his words will correspond to his thought. His face itself corresponds to his inner mood or feeling. Because heaven involves an even truer correspondence of the inner and outer, Swedenborg said the speech and the faces of angels correspond to their life even more than in persons on earth. It is said angels can know the essentials of a person's life from a few uttered words (HH 236). What angels and spirits experience around them corresponds to their interiors. In a less clear and obvious way this is true with us, too. The loving person experiences a loving world. Thieves find a world in which everyone is trying to grab from others. The holy man finds everything holy. Swedenborg even found correspondence between the spiritual and natural worlds.

The whole natural world corresponds to the spiritual world, not only the natural world in general, but also in particular. Whatever, therefore, in the natural world exists from the spiritual, is said to be its correspondent. It is to be known that the natural world exists and subsists from the spiritual world, just as an effect exists from its efficient cause. . . .

Since man is a heaven, and also a world, in least form after the image of the greatest, therefore in him there is a spiritual world and a natural world. The interiors, which belong to his mind, and relate to the understanding and will, make his spiritual world; but the exteriors, which belong to his body, and relate to its senses and actions, make his natural world. HH 90

[F]or the internal is called the spiritual man, and the external is called the natural man; and the one is as distinct from the other as heaven is from the world. All things which are done and exist in the external or natural man, are done and exist from the internal or spiritual man. HH 92

Correspondence brings levels of reality into relationship, yet it permits a multiplicity of existences. Existence itself may be said to correspond to a thought in the mind of God. All the levels of existence correspond to each other. This is true from the Lord to the celestial heaven, to the spiritual heaven, to the lowest heavens, to the world of spirits, to the interiors of man's experience, to the exteriors of experience, to the body, and to the world. Hell corresponds as opposite to heaven. Inwardly hell corresponds to the possibility of our losing track of our real nature. The Lord rules the whole of creation by correspondences, through the heavens to the world of spirits, to the innermost of man's mind, to will, understanding, outer memory and senses, to the body itself and the natural world beyond. The innermost █ mind participates in heaven and hell. Our experience is not merely an image of the whole. Inwardly, it participates in the whole. It is an example of █ there is. *HIM*

It would be an obscuring and unnecessary limitation to deal with Swedenborg as though his is only a religious or █████ psychological system. It is both at once because both are life. But let's look closer at the way the grandeur of heaven and hell come home in the interiors of personal experience.

GOD IS ONE
GOD IS A PERSON
GOD IS NOT IN SPACE.

5

The Gentle Root of Existence

There is an idea so central in Swedenborg's psychological-spiritual findings that to grasp it is to grasp the real basis of mind, or human experience *and* the nature of the worlds we are destined to experience beyond this one. The idea revolves around the concepts of love, affection, and feeling. Swedenborg had much to say of these, so we can determine quite well what he meant. It is fortunate that these gentle experiences unlock and account for the innermost of the human. Much of what he has to say can be checked in our own experience, even though what he is pointing to lies beneath thought and experience. Many will find that Swedenborg's explanation puts in good order the otherwise puzzling variability and richness of mind. It is also fortunate that these gentle ideas, in a palpable and reasonable way, account for our living in the presence of the spiritual worlds. Morever, to grasp these ideas is to grasp the essence of the design of the worlds awaiting us beyond this one.

Swedenborg's earlier life was an intellectual one, in which the scientist-engineer pieced together all the things of nature. Later he became a philosopher and pushed to the limits the possibilities of intellectual analysis and speculation. When he started examining dreams and inner processes it was apparent that he had trouble with the irrational and feeling side of experience. Gradually he came to terms with his own sensual-feeling values. The last scourging he had from the Lord before he was introduced into heaven and hell said in effect that intellect was to be servant and not master. The whole journey inward had turned his inner priorities around. The dreams, symbols, and visions he came to understand were all in a language of feeling. Correspondence and representation, or symbolization, is essentially the language of feeling, not of intellect. Intellect and reason have to be helped to even understand and accept this more primitive language of correspondence. Only feeling can find its meanings. Now we see Swedenborg after years of wandering in heaven and hell. There is no question at this point but that feeling rules and reason is her servant. Thus, one of the world's most brilliant intellects had found what is higher than intellect.

It will be recalled that heaven is essentially a state in which the most central and truest aspects of the person are opened up and lived out. From the perspective of this experience Swedenborg comes back to describe man in terms of his essentials. This provides a picture of man that is relatively unique in all the psychologies. Instead of assigning affect or feeling a secondary role, it is clearly central.

FEELING IS HIGHER THAN INTELLECT.

The Ruling Love of the Life

Swedenborg was quite aware that there are aspects of mind that are little known or understood.

Man knows nothing at all of the interior state of his mind or internal man, yet infinite things are there, not one of which comes to his knowledge. His internal of thought or internal man is his very spirit, and in it are things as infinite and innumerable as there are in his body, in fact, more numerous, for his spirit is man in its form. DP 120

This idea of the spirit being man in its form is a key one. He is pointing to the essence of humanness. In effect, humanness becomes even more human as one goes within.

Among the aspects man has trouble understanding is love itself, because while love can be felt, it does not have as definite a form as thought.

Man knows that there is such a thing as love, but he does not know what love is. He knows that there is such a thing as love from common speech, as when it is said, he loves me, a king loves his subject . . . a husband loves his wife, a mother her children . . . also, this or that one loves his country, his fellow citizens, his neighbor; and likewise of things abstracted from person, as when it is said, one loves this or that thing. But although the word love is so universally used, hardly anybody knows what love is. And because one is unable, when he reflects upon it, to form to himself any idea of thought about it, he says either that it is not anything, or that it is something flowing in . . . from . . . intercourse with others. . . . He is wholly unaware that love is his very life; not only the general life of his body, and the general life of all his thoughts, but also the life of all their particulars. . . . If you remove the affection which is from love, can you think anything or do anything? Do not thought, speech, and action grow cold in the measure in which the affection which is from love grows cold? DLW 1

The most central aspect of persons Swedenborg called the ruling or reigning love, or sometimes the love of the life. This is the core of individuality and indeed is the source of life itself. It is the same as the person's life itself. It conditions all other aspects of mind because it rules. One could hardly think of a more fundamental conception of man.

A man's very life is his love; and such as the love is, such is the life, yea, such is the whole man; but it is the ruling or reigning love that constitutes the man. This love holds in subordination many loves, which are derivations; these loves appear under a different form, but are still contained in the ruling love, and together with it constitute one kingdom. The ruling love is like their king and head; it directs them, and through them, as mediate ends, it has respect to, and intends its own end, which is the chief and ultimate end of all the loves, and it does this both directly and indirectly. It is what belongs to the ruling love which is loved above all things.

What a man loves above all things is constantly present in his thought, and also in his will, and it constitutes his veriest life. For example, he who loves wealth above all things, whether it be money or possessions, constantly turns over in his mind how he may attain it: when he does attain it, he rejoices inwardly; for his heart is in it. He who loves himself above all things, remembers himself in everything; he thinks of himself, speaks of himself, acts for the sake of himself: for his life is a life for self. HD 54–55

The love of the life is the real love. It rules over and holds in subordination many other derived loves, affections, or feelings. This ruling love contains the person's real end, or purpose in living. The influence or ruling of this essential love of the life is quite subtle and pervasive, reaching all aspects of mind.

A man has for an end what he loves above all things, and has respect to it in each and all things; it is in his will, like the hidden current of a stream which draws and bears him away even when busy with something else; for it is that which animates him. This is what one man seeks for, and also sees, in another; and according to which he either leads him or acts with him. HD 56

To underline the central role of the ruling love, Swedenborg referred to it at various times as man's life itself, his own Self, his character, the essence of the life, the soul, and the very form of his spirit. It is clear that it affects perception and interpersonal relationships.

A man is altogether of such a quality as is that which rules his life; by this he is distinguished from others; and the nature of his heaven, if he is good, is formed according to it; and also the nature

of his hell, if he is bad. It constitutes his very will, his own Self
. . . and his character; for it is the very Esse of his life, which cannot
be changed after death; because it is the man himself. HD 57

Swedenborg had found the soul in the most obvious place,
as the very life itself of man. The Greek for soul is *psy khé,*
from which came the word psychology. It isn't appropriate
to say a person *has* a soul, but rather a person *is* a soul or
a life.

As regards the soul . . . it is nothing but the man himself who
lives within the body, that is, the interior man who in this world
acts through the body, and gives life to the body. This man when
freed from the body, is called a spirit. AC 6054

Man's soul is nothing else than the love of his will and the
resulting love of his understanding; such as this love is, the whole
man is. DP 199

Is this ruling love conscious in man? All the derivatives of
it are conscious because, as we shall see, they are all the other
aspects of mind. Also, the love of the life can be inferred from
what interests or excites persons. Yet it cannot be conscious
in itself as a specific thing, because it is the general source or
basis of all human experience. There is a tantalizing aspect
to Swedenborg in that he always describes what is innermost
as most general, perfect, and most peaceful. Yet it cannot be
grasped as a specific because it is the general base or origin
of our life.

The external affections of thought manifest themselves in bodily
sensation, and sometimes in the thought of the mind, but the
internal affections of the thought from which the external exist
never make themselves manifest to man. Of these he knows no
more than a rider asleep in a carriage does of the road or than one
feels the rotation of the earth. Were you to see just one idea laid
open, you would see astounding things, more than tongue can tell.
DP 199

From the root love of the life extend ▓▓ the affections or feelings enjoyed by man. From them is derived the whole feeling life of man. Swedenborg reminded us of his skill in anatomy and symbolism in providing a beautiful image of our emotional or affective life.

By "affections" are meant continuations and derivations from love. Love may be compared to a fountain, and affections to streams flowing from it; it may also be compared to the heart, and affections to the blood vessels derived from it and continuous with it. It is, moreover, recognized that blood vessels carrying the blood from their heart re-enact the heart at every point, so that they are as it were extensions ▓▓▓. Hence the circulations of the blood from the heart along the arteries, and from the arteries into the veins, and back again into the heart. Affections also are similar, for affections are derived from love and are continuous with it, they bring uses forth ▓▓▓▓▓▓, and in these they advance from the first things of uses to their ultimates, from which they return again to the love from which they came. DLDW 22

Love comes forth and manifests itself in the uses or ▓▓ good it does. It advances in the realization of itself through ▓▓▓▓▓ uses, creating ever more its own end. In this manifesting of itself it comes to recognize its ultimate nature. Through uses it returns again to its source or nature.

Whatever is the enjoyment of one's affection is one's good, and one's truth is what is pleasant to the thought from that affection. For everyone calls that good which he feels in the love of his will to be enjoyable, and calls that truth which he then perceives in the wisdom of his understanding to be pleasant. The enjoyable and the pleasant both flow out from the life's love as water does from a spring or blood from the heart; together they are like an element or the atmosphere in which man's whole mind is. DP 195

The atmosphere of the whole mind—that is love and its derivative affection or feelings. Swedenborg also referred to affections as bonds, because they rule and control (AC 3835).

It is an existential paradox that the bonds of affections are related to freedom. In effect we feel free when we can act from our real feeling.

First, it should be known that ▓ freedom is ▓ love, so much so that love and freedom are one. As love is man's life, freedom is ▓ his life, too. For man's every enjoyment is from some love of his and has no other source, and to act from the enjoyment of one's love is to act in freedom. Enjoyment leads a man as the current bears an object along on a stream. DP 73

What it amounts to is that we know the greatest feeling of freedom if we become what we are most essentially. We are constrained in any other direction, but free to try it! This is similar to evil. By breaking existence apart, evil creates its own constraint. We are free to deviate, but there are natural mechanisms to remind us, or call us back. This very human paradox will arise again and has important mystical implications to be seen later.

Love and feeling as the life of man and the atmosphere of his inner experience have, as their first main correspondent or derivative, will. Will results in act. What one really loves, one wills and does. By this simple sequence love comes to earth in things done, what Swedenborg called uses, or goods. As is characteristic of him, what at first seems abstract or evanescent is brought to earth in the most concrete way.

Love in act is work and deed. HH 483

To love good is to will and to do good from love. HH 15

Now, as the soul of the will is love. DP 193

A man's Will is his love in form. . . . for whatever is delightful, enjoyable, pleasant, grateful, or blissful, that . . . is what the man *wills;* he says of them, in fact, that he *would like* them. . . . From all this it can be seen that Will and love, or Will and affection, with a man are one, and that his Will because it is of his love, is also his life, and is the man himself. DLDW 54

To think and to will without action, when one is able, is like a flame shut up in a vessel, which dies away; or like a seed cast upon sand, which does not grow up, but perishes with its power of germination. But to think and to will and thence to act, is like a flame which gives heat and light all around; or like a seed sown in the ground, which springs up into a tree or flower, and lives. HH 475

The love that comes to earth through man's will also generates thought and understanding. Thought or understanding is, in effect, a correspondent, or image, of feeling. It is the form that represents feeling. Feeling is the ruling source of thought, too.

Man can have no thought except from some affection of his life's love and . . . the thought is nothing other than the form of the affection. . . . The thought glides along in its enjoyment like a ship in a river current to which the skipper does not attend, attending only to the sails he spreads. DP 198

Thought is nothing but internal sight. DLW 404

The sails are like the thoughts, the manifest part of the ship's movement, but feeling is the current. Many think they rule themselves by their thoughts. I remarked earlier that in the hypnogogic state it is easy to watch the background feeling forming thoughts and words to fit it. Swedenborg was pointing toward this underlying affective or feeling layer of mind and beyond it to the ruling, most central affective direction of the individual. It will be seen that he did not put down thought as of little use; he said only that it reflects deeper processes. The affective side of thought can be felt as the tone or as the background of feeling from which thought arises. Thought gives feeling form and is part of its actualizing. If a person's thoughts are faithful to their feeling base, others can sense something of these feelings from the thoughts. It is as though feeling or good yearns to actualize as truth or act.

In the following quotations Swedenborg put together the whole sweep of the mind's operation, or man's inner experience.

The internal of thought comes out of the life's love, its affections and the perceptions from them. The external of thought is from what is in the memory, serving the life's love for confirmation and as a means to its end. From childhood to early manhood a person is in the external of thought from an affection for knowledge. . . . Later, however, his life's love is as he lives, and its affections and the perceptions from them make the internal of his thought. From his life's love comes a love of means; the enjoyments of these means and the information drawn thereby from the memory make the external of his thought. DP 105

The life's love of man rules him completely, the internal of the mind by the affections and perceptions from them, and the external by the enjoyments of the affections and of the thoughts from them. DP 106

In case there is any doubt, a little elaboration indicates that he is speaking of all aspects of mind.

There are many things pertaining to love which have received other names because they are derivatives, such as affections, desires, appetites, and their pleasures and enjoyments; and there are many things pertaining to wisdom, such as perception, reflection, recollection, thought, intention to an end; and there are many pertaining to both love and wisdom, such as consent, conclusion, and determination to action; besides others. All of these, in fact, pertain to both, but they are designated from the more prominent and nearer of the two. From these two are derived ultimately sensations, those of sight, hearing, smell, taste, and touch, with their enjoyments and pleasures. It is according to appearance that the eye sees: but it is the understanding that sees through the eye. . . . The sources of all these are love and wisdom; from which it can be seen that these two make the life of man. DLW 363

He ties together the whole in a lovely image of a tree. "The life's love is the tree; the branches with their leaves are the affections of good and truth with their perceptions; and the fruits are the enjoyments of the affections with their thoughts" (DP 107). Or he uses the imagery of love and sexual relations.

Subordinate loves or affections adjoin consorts to themselves, each its own, the interior affections consorts called perceptions, and the exterior consorts called knowledges, and each cohabits with its consorts and performs the functions of its life. . . . The union is like that of life's very being with life's coming forth, which is such that the one is nothing without the other; for what is life's being unless it is active and what is life's activity if it is not from life's very being? DP 194

The inner worlds of experience are infinitely varied and multiply endlessly: "No person enjoys an affection and perception so like another's as to be identical with it, nor ever will. Affections, moreover, may be fructified and perceptions multiplied without end" (DP 57). We can now clearly see that though Swedenborg's works look intellectual, they are colored everywhere by feeling.

Swedenborg had experienced the total ordering of mind—a rare experience! The ordering within individual minds is like the structure of societies in heaven. Since love is the key, everything is arranged in relation to it.

Truths with man are disposed and ordered in series. Those most in agreement with his loves are in the midst, those not so much in agreement are at the sides, finally those not at all in agreement are rejected to the outermost circumference. Outside this series are the things contrary to the loves. AC 5530

Swedenborg was very clear that the mind is ruled or run from the inside out. The levels of mind we usually call ourselves reflect even more basic processes. In effect, we are transcended by our own inner nature. Another way of saying it is that our conscious experience is a transcendence coming to earth in our lives; this coming to earth is our life. It would take a long careful study of the phenomenology of inner experience to prove how correct Swedenborg is in this. At this point I can only refer the reader to *The Natural Depth in Man,* which illustrates this very matter.[19]

In brief, a careful study of thought, imagery, and any discrete mental processes shows them to be embedded in affect or feeling. A very close examination shows that thought arises out of and reflects feeling. Any experimental manipulation of feeling, as in hypnotic suggestion or autosuggestion, clearly affects subsequent thought and perception. Most of this root of experience, this sea of background feeling, or atmosphere of our thought, is not really under our command. I choose to call this area the region where we are transcended. It is a region whose laws, causality, forms, and sometimes even its existence are not well known to us. Inwardly it is the aspect of ourselves that surprises and even transcends our limited outer conscious selves. It was partly this profound, phenomenological accuracy of Swedenborg that attracted me to his writings.

Swedenborg has several ways of describing this relationship of the inner to the outer aspects of mind. It has a critical bearing on the scope and real nature of humanness. It also bears on how presumptuous we can be in our conception of ourselves. And this in turn bears on whether we are creating a heaven or hell. The one who is creating a hell tends to consider the discrete doings of mind his real region of self-rule. The gentle, feeling background he overlooks or considers of little importance. The one who is creating a heaven feels he participates in processes that really transcend the limits of the little self. One can easily relate this to the shared aspect of heaven and the cut-off aspect of hell. The heavenly one feels embedded in, a participant in, a varied creation that includes the self among others. The myriads of others are the larger aspect of creation. The one designing a hell gives precedence to self over others. In effect, the effort to dominate the others, who are far greater than the self, brings the individual under the punishment of others. These are not mere happy images of spiritual processes borrowed from the social realm. The social realm is a correct, true, palpable representation of the eternal. But let us look at the emergent aspect of mind, and then later see the real inner connection with the worlds beyond this one.

Swedenborg commented on the different appearance in heaven between those who worshiped in church voluntarily and those who felt compelled to go. The inner aspect of the former looked like bright clouds, those of the latter like dark clouds. Then he says, "[I]t is plain that the internal refuses to be forced by the external and turns away. The internal can compel the external because it is like a master and the external a servant" (DP 136). It is clear that the rule is from inward to outward.

By external and internal of thought the same is meant here as by external and internal man, and by this nothing else is meant than external and internal of will and understanding, for will and understanding constitute man, and as they both manifest themselves in thoughts, we speak of external and internal of thought. And as it is the man's spirit and not his body which wills and understands and consequently thinks, external and internal are external and internal of his spirit. The body's activity in speech or deed is only an effect from the external and internal of man's spirit, for the body is so much obedience. DP 103

The body does nothing of itself, but from its spirit which is in it. HD 46

In the Internal there are thousands and thousands of things, which in the External appear as one general thing. Therefore thought and perception are the clearer as they are more interior. From this it follows ·that a man ought to be in internal things. HD 47

All those who are in an External apart from an Internal, that is, with whom the spiritual Internal has been closed, are in hell. HD 47

The Natural is a kind of face in which interior things behold themselves; and it is thus that man thinks. HD 48

Internal things are those which are represented, and external things those which represent. HD 262

The internal of thought comes out of the life's love, its affections and the perceptions from them. The external of thought is from what is in the memory, serving the life's love for confirmation and as means to its end. DP 105

The memory here includes knowledge of language. Spoken thought comes from the external of memory to serve the inner affective or emotional aspect of mind.

Swedenborg occasionally made a direct appeal to the reader to check out something in his own experience, such as the following:

From an unclouded rationality anyone can see or grasp that without the appearance that it is his own a man cannot be in any affection to know or to understand. Every joy and pleasure, thus everything of the will, is from an affection of some love. Who can wish to know or to understand anything except that an affection of his takes pleasure in it? Who can feel this pleasure unless what he is affected by seems to be his? DP 76

Swedenborg's "unclouded rationality" would correspond to a careful phenomenological study that attempts to see and describe what exists in mind. "That a man possesses external and internal thought is also plain in that from his interior thought he can behold the exterior thought, can reflect on it, too, and judge whether or not it is evil" (DP 104).

There is a correspondence between the internal thought or spirit of man and the externals of thought. Swedenborg also described this as part of a metaphysical principle that runs through the whole of creation. The ultimate end of all things generates a cause that results in effects. In mind the love of the life is the end. It generates causes from which are the affections and the perceptions serving the love of the life. The resulting effects are the externals of thought and the body's actions. A person's real end shows in what he does. In religious terms, love results in charity. End, cause, effect is the principle that has also been described as correspondence between levels of creation. The end is the inmost aspect, the effect, the outermost.

The human mind dwells always in the Trine called end, cause, and effect. If one of these is lacking, the mind is not possessed of its life. An affection of the will is the initiating end; the thought of the understanding is the efficient cause; and bodily action, utterance or external sensation is the effect from the end by means of the thought. Anyone sees that the human mind is not possessed of its life when it is only in an affection of the will and in naught besides, or when it is only in effect. The mind has no life from one of these separately, but from the three together. DP 178

This manifesting through levels of our own existence is what we call living.

Although the internal contains a person's highest potential and the ultimate aim of the life, it also contains the possibility of error, or getting lost. This possibility arises out of our freedom to try things and to judge for ourselves. It is clear that Swedenborg saw this ultimate shaping of the person as requiring freedom. The external cannot constrain the internal, which is its source. The external is the coming to earth, the manifesting of the internal. The internal is the ultimate of personal freedom and, as we shall see later, the connection with heaven. The experiences of life are the manifesting of the internal. Man's judging, based on experiences, is the means by which he sets his values, what he stands for.

No one is reformed in a state of fear because fear takes away freedom and reason or liberty and rationality. Love opens the mind's interiors but fear closes them, and when they are closed man thinks little and only what comes to the lower mind or to the senses. All fears that assail the lower mind have this effect. . . . Fear can never invade the internal of thought; this is always in freedom, being in a man's life-love. . . . The fear that invades the external of thought and closes the internal is chiefly fear of losing [social] standing or profit. DP 139

There can be a real conflict between the external and internal. The more the person acts presumptuously against the internal, the more he sets up a conflict with his own inner source. Liberty or freedom resides in the internal, thus to stand against the internal is to block one's own freedom. Regarding the inner and the outer:

They act separately when a man speaks and acts from the external of his thought otherwise than he thinks and wills inwardly; they act conjointly when he speaks and acts as he thinks and wills. The latter is common with the sincere, the former with the insincere. Inasmuch as the internal and the external of the mind are so distinct, the internal can even fight with the external and by combat drive it to compliance.

Now as man is man by virtue of the internal of his thought, for this is his very spirit, obviously he compels himself when he compels the external of his thought to comply or to receive the enjoyments of his affections. DP 145

Man is free to think as he pleases to the end that his life's love may emerge from its hiding-place into the light of the understanding, and since he would not otherwise know anything of his own evil. DP 281

The conflict between the higher internal and the lower external Swedenborg described as temptation, or combat. The struggle itself is necessary so that a person may become conscious and decide his own values, thereby shaping his ultimate or eternal existence. We make what will always be. As the inner and outer come to act as one, the individual comes to experience the peace and freedom that is the life of the inner. One might call this integration, mental health, or well-being.

With those in a heavenly love . . . internal and external man make one, when they speak, and they are aware of no difference. Their life's love, with its affections of good and the perceptions of truth from these, is like a soul in what they think and then say and do. DP 110

All this has bearing on marital relationships. In spite of not being married, Swedenborg pondered long on the relationship of male to female. One of his last published works, *Marital Love,* issued when he was eighty years old, is considered by many of his followers one of his greatest works. He was frank enough on the intimate aspects of marriage that this work was banned in Boston for a time! Yet by modern standards this book seems entirely elevated. He wanted to get at the psychological and spiritual aspects of the union of persons. He answered the question of whether sex has any role in heaven.

Love for the sex continues after death with every person as it was inwardly, that is, such as it was in the interior will and thought in the world. All one's love follows one after death, for love is the *esse* of man's life. The ruling love, which is the head of the rest, and subordinate loves along with it, persist with man to eternity. Loves persist because strictly they are of man's spirit, and of the body from the spirit, and after death the human becomes a spirit, and thus takes his love with him. . . . As for sexual love, it is the universal love, having been put by creation in man's very soul, which is his whole essence, and this for the sake of the propagation of the race. This love in particular remains, because a man after death is a man and a woman is a woman, and there is nothing in soul, mind or body, which is not masculine in the male and feminine in the female. The two have been so created, moreover, that they seek after conjunction, yes, to be one; this striving is the love of the sex, which precedes marital love. A conjunctive inclination which has been inscribed on each and all things of man and woman certainly cannot be blotted out and perish with the body. ML 46

Sexual love he saw as a desire to join with many; marital love is a higher and purer love that needs only one. Maleness and femaleness he saw as no small accident of fate: male and female differ even in the subtlest aspects of the inner life. In fact, he saw the differences in the male and female body as representative of the inner. The male is harder, more linear, and even sexually is a thrust outward. The female is softer, more rounded, nurturant, and even sexually is softer and more inward. Feminine males and masculine women would be variants of them. In effect the male is trying to unite with his own potential love aspect in women, and a woman is attempting to unite with her wisdom aspect in a man. There is a basic difference in the male and female approach to reality. "To perceive from understanding is masculine, and to do so from love is feminine" (ML 168).

Swedenborg may reflect a little of the masculine chauvinism of his time. Microscopes had only recently been developed; genetics had not been founded. And Swedenborg, like most scientists of his day, probably felt that the whole seed and heredity was from the father. The mother was simply a vessel for the development of this seed. But if we can overlook this, we can see Swedenborg reaching for the real inward nature of love and marital relationships, puzzling out the inward necessity that binds men and women together. I recall one lovely description in which he came upon a truly married couple in heaven. They looked like one person till he got close enough to see they were two. He remarked that man and wife meet again in heaven and see if they were truly joined inwardly. Often they are not, and go their separate ways and find new and eternally compatible spouses! Swedenborg said that Christ's statement that there is no marriage in heaven (Luke XX, 27–28) referred to union with God, that can never take place unless a foundation is laid in this life (ML 41).

He saw in sex and love a deeper principle that operated through all creation. Swedenborg often described it as the marriage of good and truth. Love is the good seeking to be made actual in truth or reality. The scholar Iungerich felt Swedenborg was describing the divine as creator (male) and sustainer of existence (female).[20] These are primal opposites very much like the yin-yang of the Chinese.[21] The creator aspect shows in the male impregnating the female, while the sustaining aspect shows in the female bearing, nursing, and caring for the child.

The Connection with Heaven

So far we have not shown any real connecting link with heaven. It is clear that by the style and quality of his life the individual sets his eternal condition. But during this life on earth is there a more immediate link with the worlds beyond? There is, but it is not explicit, so that many who have studied Swedenborg would not know the link.

As we saw, in Swedenborg's terms the innermost of the individual is the love of the life, or the ruling love. Out of this emanate the affections, feelings, or inner tendencies, which are the ruling background of the explicit aspects of consciousness. In *Heaven and Hell* Swedenborg said that spirits of heaven and hell interact with man. Yet this interaction is not usually apparent, nor was it meant to be. If spirits interact inwardly in the mind of individuals, it takes place in our inner feelings. At first sight this seems like a strange idea, that spirits are present in our feelings. But as we examine its implications it becomes much more reasonable. The first step is to see that spirits and affections are the same thing. This is a consequence of their coming into their real inner tendencies. It is more accurate to see them as their inner ruling tendencies than to view them in their individual identities as Joe or Mary. This is part of their being beyond space and time.

[E]very angel is an affection and is also a use. DLDW 24

[F]or spirits are affections, and therefore in a human form similar to their affections. HH 517

As all spirits and angels, then, are affections, the whole angelic heaven is nothing but the love of all the affections of good and the attendant wisdom of all the perceptions of truth. DP 61

Combine with this the fact that a person inwardly is essentially his affection or life's love and really has contact with heaven and hell:

[A] man's spirit is nothing else than affection, and that consequently after death he becomes an affection, an angel of heaven if he is an affection for a good use, a spirit of hell if an affection for an evil use. This is why the entire heaven is distinguished into societies according to the genera and species of affections; and hell likewise, in an opposite order. Consequently when you speak of affections, or of societies in the spiritual world, it is the same. DLDW 21

The internal man is what is called the spiritual man, because it is in the light of heaven, which light is spiritual; and the external man is what is called the natural man, because it is in the light of the world, which light is natural. The man whose Internal is in the light of heaven, and whose External is in the light of the world, is a spiritual man as to both; but the man whose Internal is not in the light of heaven, but only the light of the world in which also is his External, is a natural man as to both. It is the spiritual man, who, in the Word, is called a living man, and the natural man who is called a dead man.

The man whose Internal is in the light of heaven, and his External in the light of the world, thinks both spiritually and naturally, but in the latter case his spiritual thought flows into his natural thought, and is there perceived.

The internal spiritual man, regarded in himself, is an angel of heaven; and even while living in the body, is in association with angels, although he is not aware of it, and after his separation from the body, he comes among angels. HD 38–40

When angels are with men, they dwell, as it were, in their affections. HH 391

Not only are we inwardly affections, which join us to societies in heaven and hell which are also affections, but Swedenborg also said specifically that spirits interact with us.

With every man there are good spirits and evil spirits: by good spirits man has conjunction with heaven, and by evil spirits with hell. These spirits are in the world of spirits, which is in the midst between heaven and hell. . . . When these spirits come to man, they enter into all his memory, and thence into all his thought; evil spirits, into those things of the memory and thought which are evil, but good spirits, into those things of the memory and thought which are good. The spirits do not know at all that they are with man, but when they are with him they believe that all things of his memory and thought are their own; neither do they see man, because things which are in our solar world are not objects of their sight. HH 292

Later, when we examine psychotic hallucinations, we will see a surprising contemporary confirmation of this assertion. What Swedenborg described fits perfectly with careful phenomenological studies of inner experience.[22] The most primitive level of mental functioning we can observe is feelings or affections. Thought and perception follow their pattern. Swedenborg adds that spirits are affections and are present inwardly in our feelings. Everyone has good and evil spirits with him. Man is the free space poised between these opposite possibilities. Moreover, we don't have just any old spirits with us, only those that reflect our inward feeling potentials. A man of a given dark disposition or inner tendency would have a spirit of like nature with him. *There is no real way of distinguishing our own potentialities and the potentialities of spirits with us.* As Albert Einstein once remarked, it is not appropriate to see as separate, things which cannot be distinguished. The spirits with us and our affective potentialities are the same thing. Or, to enlarge the statement, some aspects of the spiritual worlds beyond this one are already real in us now. Or, to put this yet another way, there is a correspondence between the spiritual worlds and the mind of man. The specific line of correspondence in the individual is through the affective spirits with him, into his affects and thence into all other levels of mind. But this is really how the Lord rules, through the world of spirits to the mind of man:

[Man] believes that all things in him in general and particular follow in natural order, and that there is nothing higher which directs them, although the fact is this, that all things in general and particular are arranged by means of spirits and angels with him, and that hence come all states and changes of states, and thus they are directed by the Lord towards ends to eternity, which ends the Lord alone foresees. That this is the case has been made known to me most clearly by the experience of several years; it has also been given to me to know and observe what spirits and angels were with me, and what states they induced; and this I can firmly assert, that all states, even to their smallest particulars, came from this source, and that they are thus directed by the Lord. AC 2796

It may be difficult for some to see, but Swedenborg's explanation of mind as based on the presence of spirits is not observably different from the modern dynamic theories of the nature of mind, formed two centuries after him. In the older psychoanalysis, the mind is based in unconscious processes which are primarily affective.[23] Swedenborg said these inner affections are unconscious and rule. The added element Swedenborg brought to it is a basing of these unconscious affects in spiritual worlds beyond this one. When we examine the strange world of psychotic hallucinations we will see that Swedenborg's description of the process is even more impressive than that of psychoanalysis.

Theories of mind shift with the trend of the times. Most current theories see the most critical tendencies of the individual as reflecting the interpersonal relations with significant others.[24] In effect, we introject or take on the ways of the significant others we are associated with. This social introject is carried within as affective potentialities for certain kinds of behavior. Again, there is no really good way of distinguishing this from what Swedenborg has to say. Swedenborg is also saying we reflect affective potentialities within. On a clinical or phenomenological level there isn't much to distinguish Swedenborg's conception of mind from modern theories. (I don't regard this as proven here. Such a proof would require an extensive study in itself, especially since there are hundreds of modern theories.)

It is only when we search beyond what is easily observed to root causes that Swedenborg's conception of mind is radically different. He took into account whole orders of existence that have no place in most modern theories. His is really a theological psychology. The worlds of God, heaven and hell, and man are too intimately interrelated to Swedenborg for him to try to isolate them from each other profitably.

Ordinarily I would say there is hardly any satisfactory way to check on the heaven and hell aspect of Swedenborg's findings, except that I accidently stumbled upon a surprising confirmation.

6

The Presence of Spirits in Madness

By an extraordinary series of circumstances I seem to have found a confirmation for one of Emanuel Swedenborg's more unusual findings: that man's life involves an interaction with a hierarchy of spirits. This interaction is normally not conscious, but perhaps in some cases of mental illness it has become conscious.

For sixteen years I worked as a clinical psychologist in one of the country's better mental hospitals (Mendocino State Hospital, Ukiah, California; now closed). Out of both my professional role and human interest I examined thousands of mentally ill persons. An accidental discovery in 1964 permitted me to get a much more detailed and accurate picture of psychotic hallucinations than had previously been possi-

*This chapter is an adaptation of an article, "The Presence of Spirits in Madness," in the *New Philosophy* 70 (1967):461–477; in a Swedenborg foundation pamphlet of the same name, 1968; and as "Hallucinations as the World of Spirits," *Psychedelic Review* 11 (1971):59–70. My findings in hallucinations are described in greater detail in Chapter 10 of *The Natural Depth in Man*, but without the comparison to Swedenborg.

ble. Though I gradually noticed similarities between patients' reports and Swedenborg's description of the relationships of man to spirits, it was only three years after all my major findings on hallucinations had been made that the striking similarity between the two became apparent to me. I then collected as many details as possible of his description. I found that Swedenborg's system not only is an almost perfect fit with patients' experiences, but even more impressively, it accounts for otherwise quite puzzling aspects of hallucinations.

Mentally ill persons are out of sorts with their environment and need supervision, care, or restraint for their protection or the welfare of others. If they are very disturbed or apparently responding to invisible others, the staff may decide they are hallucinating. Most hallucinating people conceal this experience because they know it is unusual and may indicate madness. At best our patients would tell us of a few striking hallucinations from the past. An unusually cooperative patient led me to ask if I could talk directly with her hallucinations. I did, and she gave me their immediate response. I had stumbled upon a way to get a much richer picture of the inner world of hallucinations.

I began to look for patients who could distinguish between their own thoughts and the things heard and seen. Some of the more deteriorated psychotics couldn't distinguish between themselves and hallucinations any longer. The ego had been overrun with alien forces so that there were no clear distinctions. My patients were in relatively good condition. The patients were told that I simply wanted to get as accurate a description of their experiences as possible. I held out no hope for recovery or special reward. It soon became apparent that many were embarrassed by what they saw and heard. Also, they knew their experiences were not shared by others, and some were even concerned that their reputations would suffer if they revealed the obscene nature of their voices. It took some care to make the patients comfortable enough to reveal their experience honestly. A further complication was that the voices were sometimes frightened of me and themselves needed reassurance. They felt that a psychologist might want to kill them, which was, in a sense, true! I struck up a relationship with both the patient and the persons he saw and heard. I would question these other persons directly, and instructed the patient to give a word-for-word account of what the voices answered or what was seen. In this way I could hold long dialogues with a patient's hallucinations and record both my questions and their answers. My method was that of phenomenology. My only purpose was to describe the patient's experiences as accurately as possible. The reader may notice I treat the hallucinations as realities—that is what they are to the patient. My acting this way was part of my attempt to get as close as possible to the experience as these people felt it. I would work with a patient for as little as one hour or as long as several months of inquiry, where the hallucinated world was complex enough.

Why should one believe what these patients report? The patients cooperated with me only because I was honestly trying to understand their experiences. Most of my subjects seemed fairly sensible except for their hallucinations, which invaded and interfered with their lives. On several occasions I talked with hallucinations that the patient himself did not really understand. This was especially true when I dealt with what will be described as the higher-order hallucinations, which can be symbolically rich beyond the patient's own understanding. There was great consistency in what was reported independently by different patients. I have no reason to doubt they were reporting real experiences. They seemed to be honest people as puzzled as I was to explain what was happening to them. The differences in the experiences of schizophrenics, alcoholics, the brain-damaged, and senile were not as striking as the similarities.

One consistent finding was that patients felt they had contact with another world or order of beings. Most thought these other persons were living. All objected to the term "hallucination." Each coined his own term, such as the Other Order, the Eavesdroppers, air phone, etc.

For most individuals the hallucinations came on suddenly. One woman was working in the garden when an unseen man addressed her. Another man described sudden loud noises and voices he heard while riding in a bus. Most were frightened, and adjusted with difficulty to this new experience. All the patients described voices as having the quality of a real voice, sometimes louder, sometimes softer, than normal voices. The experience they described was quite unlike thoughts or fantasies: when things are seen they appear fully real. For instance, a patient described being awakened one night by air force officers calling him to the service of his country. He got up and was dressing when he noticed their insignia wasn't quite right, then their faces altered. With this he knew they were of the Other Order and struck one hard in the face. He hit the wall and injured his hand. He could not distinguish them from reality until he noticed the insignia. One woman saw Egypt's President Gamal Abdel Nasser sitting in a chair in my office. When I respectfully passed my hand down the back of the chair, my hand was blotted out for her by the body of President Nasser. Most patients soon realize that they are having experiences that others do not share, and for this reason learn to keep quiet about them. Many suffer insults, threats, and attacks for years from voices with no one around them aware of it.

In my dialogues with patients I learned of two orders of experience, borrowing from the voices themselves, called the higher and the lower order. Lower-order voices are similar to drunken bums at a bar who like to tease and torment just for the fun of it. They suggest lewd acts and then scold the patient for considering them. They find a weak point of conscience and work on it interminably. For instance, one man heard voices teasing him for three years over a ten-cent debt he had already paid. They call the patient every conceivable name, suggest every lewd act, steal memories or ideas right out of consciousness, threaten death, and work on the patient's credibility in every way. For instance, they brag that they will produce some disaster on the morrow and then claim honor for one in the daily paper. They suggest foolish acts, such as to raise your right hand in the air and stay that way, and tease if he does it and threaten him if he doesn't. The lower order can work for a long time to possess some part of the patient's body. Several worked on one patient's ear and he seemed to grow deafer. One voice worked two years to capture a patient's eye, which went visibly out of alignment. Many patients have heard loud and clear voices plotting their death for weeks on end, an apparently nerve-wracking experience. One patient saw a noose around his neck that was tied to "I don't know what," while voices plotted his death by hanging. They threaten pain and can cause felt pain as a way of enforcing their power. The most devastating experience of all is to be shouted at constantly by dozens of voices. When this occurred the patient became grossly disturbed and had to be sedated. The vocabulary and range of ideas of the lower order is limited, but they have a persistent will to destroy. They invade every nook and cranny of privacy, work on every weakness and belief, claim awesome powers, lie, make promises, and then undermine the patient's will. They never have a personal identity, though they accept most names or identities given them. They either conceal or have no awareness of personal memories. Though they claim to be separate identities they will reveal no detail that might help to trace them as separate individuals. Their voice quality can change or shift, leaving the patient quite confused as to who might be speaking.

When identified as some friend known to the patient, they can assume this voice quality perfectly. For convenience many patients call them by nicknames, such as "Fred," "The Doctor," or "The Old-Timer." I've heard it said by the higher-order voices that the purpose of the lower order is to illuminate all of the person's weaknesses. They do that admirably and with infinite patience. To make matters worse they hold out promises to patients and even give helpful-sounding advice, only to catch the patient in some weakness. Even with the patient's help I found the lower order difficult to relate to because of their disdain for me as well as the patient.

The limited vocabulary and range of ideas of the lower order is striking. A few ideas can be repeated endlessly. One voice just said "hey" for months while the patient tried to figure out whether "hey" or "hay" was meant. Even when I was supposedly speaking to an engineer that a woman heard, the engineer was unable to do any more arithmetic than simple sums and multiplication the woman had memorized. The lower-order voices seem incapable of sequential reasoning. Though they often claim to be in some distant city, they cannot report more than the patient sees, hears, or remembers. They seem imprisoned in the lowest level of the patient's mind, giving no real evidence of a personal world or of any higher-order thinking or experiencing.

All of the lower order are irreligious or antireligious. Some actively interfered with the patients' religious practices. Most patients considered them as ordinary living people, though to one patient they appeared as conventional devils and referred to themselves as demons. In a few instances they referred to themselves as from hell. Occasionally they would speak through the patient so that the patient's voice and speech would be directly those of the voices. Sometimes they acted through the patient. One of my female patients was found going out the hospital gate arguing loudly with her male voice that she didn't want to leave, but he was insisting.

Like many others, this particular hallucination claimed to be Jesus Christ, but his bragging and argumentativeness rather gave him away as of the lower order. Sometimes the lower order is embedded in physical concerns, as in the case of a lady who was tormented by experimenters painfully treating her joints to prevent arthritis. She held out hope that they were helping her, though it was apparent to any onlooker they had all but destroyed her life as a free and intelligent person.

In direct contrast stand the rarer higher-order hallucinations. In quantity they make up perhaps a fifth or less of the patients' experiences. This contrast may be illustrated by the experience of one man. He had heard the lower order arguing for a long while about how they would murder him. He also had a light come to him at night, like the sun. He knew it was a different order because the light respected his freedom and would withdraw if it frightened him. In contrast, the lower order worked against his will and would attack if it could sense fear in him. This rarer higher order seldom speaks, whereas the lower order can talk endlessly. The higher order is much more likely to be symbolic, religious, supportive, genuinely instructive; it can communicate directly with the inner feelings of the patient. It is similar to Jung's archetypes, whereas the lower order is like Freud's id. I've learned to help the patient approach the higher order because of its great power to broaden the individual's values. When the man was encouraged to approach his friendly sun he entered a world of powerful numinous experiences, in some ways more frightening than the murderers who plotted his death. In one scene he found himself at the bottom of a long corridor with doors at the end behind which raged the powers of hell. He was about to let out these powers when a very powerful and impressive Christlike figure appeared and by direct mind-to-mind communication counseled him to leave the doors closed and follow him into other experiences that were therapeutic for him. In another instance the higher order appeared to a man as a lovely woman who entertained him while showing him thousands of symbols. Though the patient was a high school–educated gas pipe fitter, his female vision showed a knowledge of religion and myth far beyond the patient's comprehension. At the end of a very rich dialogue with her (the patient reporting her symbols and responses), the patient asked for just a clue as to what she and I were talking about. Another example is that of a black man who gave up being useful and lived as a drunken thief. In his weeks of hallucinations the higher order carefully instructed him on the trials of all minority groups and left him with the feeling he would like to do something for minorities.

Some patients experience both the higher and lower orders at various times and feel caught between a private heaven and hell. Many only know the attacks of the lower order. The higher order claims power over the lower order and, indeed, shows it at times, but not enough to give peace of mind to most patients. The higher order itself has indicated that the usefulness of the lower order is to illustrate and make conscious the patients' weaknesses and faults.

Though I could say much more on what the patients reported and quote extensively from dialogues with hallucinations, this is the substance of my findings. I was very early impressed by the overall similarities of what patients reported even though they had no contact with each other. After twenty patients there wasn't much more to be learned. I was also impressed by the similarity to the relatively little shown in the biblical accounts of possession. These patients might well be going through experiences quite similar to what others felt centuries ago.

Several things stood out as curious and puzzling. The lower order seemed strangely prevalent and limited. In the face of their claim of separate identity, their concealing or

GOD-MAN

not knowing any fact (birthplace, schooling, name, personal history) that would set them apart was unusual. Their malevolence and persistence in undermining the patient was striking. And why would they consistently be nonreligious and antireligious? Just the mention of religion provoked anger or derision from them. In contrast, the higher order appeared strangely gifted, sensitive, wise, and religious. They did not conceal identity but rather would have an identity above the human. For instance, a lady of the higher order was described as "an emanation of the feminine aspect of the Divine." When I implied she was Divine she took offense. She herself was not Divine but she was an emanation of the Divine. I couldn't help but begin to feel I was dealing with some kind of contrasting polarity of good and evil. The patients' accounts of voices trying to seize for their own some part of the body, such as eye, ear, or tongue, had a strangely ancient ring to it. Some people might suspect that my manner of questioning fed back to the patients what I wanted to hear, but I had occasion to address an audience of patients and staff in the hospital on hallucinations. Afterward many patients I had not met came up and pressed my hand and said I had described their experiences too. As incredible as it may seem, I'm inclined to believe the above is a roughly accurate account of many patients' hallucinatory experiences.

Though I had read Swedenborg, the similarity between his account of heaven and hell and patients' experiences was not immediately apparent to me. His doctrine regarding spirits I could neither affirm or deny. It was the clear and persistent reports from patients of attempts at possession that first reminded me of biblical accounts and later of Swedenborg.

Not much was known of madness two centuries ago. Swedenborg did speculate on the matter. He sometimes described it as being too involved in one's own fantasies (SD 1752), and sometimes ascribed it to pride in one's own

INTELLIGENCE

spiritual madness [AC 10227]). He gave much description of possession by spirits and what they did. Hallucinations look most like what Swedenborg described under the general headings of obsessions (to be caught in false ideas) and possession (to have alien spirits acting into one's own thought, feelings, or even into one's bodily acts [HH 257]). He indicated that normally there is a barrier between these spiritual entities and man's own consciousness. He was describing a hallucination, and the dangers involved:

> The speech of an angel or spirit with man is heard as sonorously as the speech of man with man, yet not by others who stand near, but by himself alone. The reason is that the speech of an angel or spirit flows first into man's thought and by an internal way into his organ of hearing thus affecting it from within. . . .
>
> To speak with spirits at this day is rarely granted, because it is dangerous, for then the spirits know that they are with man, otherwise they do not know it, and evil spirits are such, that they regard man with deadly hatred, and desire nothing more than to destroy him, both soul and body. This in fact is done with those who have indulged much in phantasies, so as to remove themselves from the delights proper to the natural man. Some also who lead a solitary life occasionally hear spirits speaking with them. HH 248–249

If evil spirits knew they were with man they would do all sorts of things to torment him and destroy his life. What he described looks remarkably like my own findings on the lower-order hallucinations. Let us consider lower-order hallucinations and possession by evil spirits together. You will recall that I said lower-order hallucinations act against the patient's will, and are extremely verbal, persistent, attacking, and malevolent. They use trickery to deceive the patient as to their powers, and threaten, cajole, entreat, and undermine in every conceivable way. These are all characteristics of possession by evil spirits, which takes place when the spirits are no longer unconscious, but have some awareness of themselves as separate entities and act into consciousness.

REPEAT

It is not clear how the awareness barrier between spirits and man is broken. In Swedenborg's case he apparently did it deliberately with his practice of inward concentration and trances. Swedenborg described his experience as a special gift from the Lord, in which he could be tormented like others and yet be protected from harm (SD 3963). In the context of his whole system of thought, one would surmise this inner barrier of awareness is penetrated when the person habitually withdraws from social usefulness into inner fantasy and pride. This would conform to contemporary social withdrawal, which is the earliest aspect of schizophrenia. I am relatively certain that religious faith alone doesn't prevent hallucinations because many patients try to save themselves by religious practices. Observation would suggest useful social acts, charity, would come closer to preventing schizophrenia.

All of Swedenborg's observations on the effect of evil spirits entering man's consciousness conform to my findings. The most fundamental one is that they attempt to destroy him (AC 6192, 4227). They can cause anxiety or pain (AC 6202). They speak in man's native tongue (ML 326, DP 135). (The only instances I could find where hallucinations seemed to know a language other than the patient's were in the higher order.) They seek to destroy conscience (AC 1983) and seem to be against every higher value. For instance, they interfere with reading or religious practices. They suggest acts against the patient's conscience and, if refused, threaten, make them seem plausible, or do anything to overcome the patient's resistance. Swedenborg said these spirits can impersonate and deceive (SD 2687). This accounts for one puzzling aspect. Patients say voices can shift voice quality and identity as they speak, making it impossible to identify. Or, if a patient treats them as some known individual, they will act like him. They lie (SD 1622). Most patients who have experienced voices for any length of time come to recognize this. They tell a patient he will die tomorrow and yet he lives. They claim to be anyone, including the Holy Spirit (HH 249). It took some while for a woman patient to come to realize the male voice in her probably was not Jesus Christ, as it claimed. She considered him sick and proceeded to counsel this voice, which improved and left her! He claimed he could read my mind, but I showed her by a simple experiment that he couldn't. *CATHOLIC CHURCH*

When spirits begin to speak with man, he must beware lest he believe them in anything; for they say almost anything; things are fabricated by them, ~~and~~ they lie; for if they were permitted to relate what heaven is, and how things are in the heavens, they would tell ~~so~~ many lies, and indeed with a solemn affirmation, that man would be astonished. . . . They are extremely fond of fabricating: and whenever any subject of discourse is proposed, they think that they know it, and give their opinions one after another, one in one way, and another in another, altogether as if they knew; and if a man listens ~~and believes~~, they press on, ~~and~~ deceive, and seduce in divers ways. SD 1622

Though most patients tend to recognize this, many still put faith in ~~their~~ voices and remain caught by them. For instance, one lady felt a group of scientists, including a physician and engineer, was doing important but painful experiments on the ends of her bones. Even though I couldn't find a trace of medical knowledge in the physician or any mathematical ability above simple sums in the engineer, she continued to believe in them.

Many voices have indicated they will take over the world, or have already done so, which bit of bragging Swedenborg noticed too (SD 4476). I asked one lower-order voice what his real aims were. He candidly said, "Fight, screw, win the world." They can suggest and try to enforce strange acts in the patient and then condemn him for compliance.

Man does not produce anything false and evil from himself, but it is the evil spirits with him who produce it, and at the same time make the man believe that he does it of himself. Such is their malignity. And what is more, at the moment when they are infusing and compelling this belief, they accuse and condemn him, as I can confirm from many experiences. AC 761

THE CHURCH (BAPTIST·HUT) CONDEMNS GOD-MAN

They draw attention to things sexual or simply filthy (SD 2852) and then proceed to condemn the person for noticing them. They often refer to the person as just an automation or machine.

EVIL CHURCH FOLKS

Thus men walk about as machines; they are nothing in the eyes of spirits; and if they know one to be a man, and also a spirit, they would look upon him as an inanimate machine, while the man all the time supposes himself to be thinking, and the spirit nothing. SD 3633

SPIRIT + TIME

That a person is an automaton is a common psychotic delusion, arising out of hallucinated experience. In the normal condition these spirits cannot see and hear the world (AC 1880), but in mental illness they can (SD 3963). For instance I was able to give the Rorschach inkblot test to a patient's voices separately from the patient's own responses. Incidentally, the lower-order hallucinations appeared to be much sicker than the patient. Since I could talk with them through the patient's hearing, they could hear what the patient heard. Though they seem to have the same sensory experience as the patient, I could find no evidence they could see or hear things remote from the patient's senses, as they often claimed.

There are a number of peculiar traits of the lower-order hallucinations on which Swedenborg threw light. If voices are merely the patient's unconscious coming forth, I would have no reason to expect them to be particularly for or against religion. Yet the lower order can be counted on to give its most scurrilous comments to any suggestion of religion. They either totally deny any afterlife or oppose God and all religious practices (AC 6197). Once I asked if they were spirits, and they answered, "The only spirits around here are in bottles" (followed by raucous laughter). To Swedenborg it is their opposition to God, religion, and all that this implies that makes them what they are.

Another peculiar finding is that the lower-order hallucinations were somehow bound to and limited within the patient's own experiences (AC 796f). The lower order could not reason sequentially or think abstractly as could the higher order. Also, it seemed limited within the patient's own memory. For instance, one group of voices could attack the patient only for things he had recalled since they invaded him; and they were most anxious to get any dirt to use against him. Swedenborg throws light on this when he indicates that one class of evil spirits is limited to man's memory (HH 292, 298). This accounts for ██ memory limitation, its lack of sequential ███████ reasoning, and its ███████ repetitiveness. As I indicated earlier, it is not uncommon for voices to attack a person for years over a single past guilt. It also accounts for the ████ verbal quality of the lower order as against the higher order's frequent inability to speak ████ (ML 326).

Swedenborg indicated the possibility of spirits acting through the subject (AC 5990), which was to possess him. This I have occasionally seen. For instance the man who thought he was Christ within a woman sometimes spoke through her, at which times her voice was unnaturally rough and deep. She also had trouble with him dressing at the same time she was, because she would be caught in the incongruities of doing two different acts at once.

Another peculiar finding that Swedenborg unintentionally explained is my consistent experience that lower-order hallucinations act as though they are separate individuals and yet can in no way reveal even a trace of personal identity. Nor can they produce anything more than was in the patient's memory. This strange but consistent finding is clarified by Swedenborg's account. These lower-order spirits enter a man's memory and lose all personal memory. Their personal memory was taken off at their death, leaving their more interior aspects. That they discover they are other than the man allows obsession and possession to take place and accounts for their claiming separate identity and convincing the patient of this. But their actual lack of personal memory comes from their taking on the patient's own.

It may be that in the deeper degree of schizophrenia the spirits have taken on more of their own memory. Swedenborg said that this would lead man to believe he had done what he had not done (AC 2478, HH 256). For instance, delusional ideas are a belief in what has not occurred. Some patients spoke of themselves as dead and buried and their present identity as of another person. "For were spirits to retain their corporeal memory, they would so far obsess man, that he would have no more self-control or be in the enjoyment of his life, than one actually obsessed" (SD 3783). I am just guessing at this point that the most serious mental disorders—where a person is totally out of contact and jabbers to himself and gesticulates strangely—are instances where these spirits have more memory and act more thoroughly through the person. It is then symbolically accurate that the patient is dead and someone else lives.

I deliberately looked for some discrepancy between my patients' experiences and Swedenborg's descriptions. I appeared to have found it in the number of spirits who were with one patient. Patients may have three or four most frequent voices, but they can experience a number of different people. Swedenborg said there are usually only two good and two evil spirits with a person (AC 904, 5470, 5848, 6189). He also gave instances where spirits come in clouds of people at a time (SD 4546). I later learned that where there is a split between the internal and external experience of a person, as in schizophrenia, there can be many spirits with a person (SD 160). Also, as patients' voices themselves have described the situation, one spirit can be the subject or voice of many (HH 601). This was the case with the lady who had the researchers working on her bones. They themselves were in a kind of hierarchy and represented many. Only the lowest few members of the hierarchy became known to the patient and myself. Swedenborg referred to such spirits as the subjects of many.

Both Swedenborg and medieval literature spoke of the aim of spirits to possess and control some part of a patient's body (SD 1751, 2656, 4910, 5569). Parts involved in my observations have been the ear, eye, tongue, and genitals. Medieval literature speaks of intercourse between a person and his or her possessing spirit, giving these spirits the names "incubi" and "succubi," depending on their sex. One female patient described her sexual relations with her male spirit as both more pleasurable and more inward than normal intercourse. Swedenborg made it clear that those who enter the affections or emotions enter thereby into all things of the body. These more subtle possessions are more powerful than simply having voices talking to one, and can easily account for affective psychoses where there is a serious mood change (SD 5981). One older German woman was depressed by tiny devils who tormented her in her genital region and made her feel the horror of hell.

Both possession and the experimental way in which Swedenborg entered these experiences is illustrated by the following:

It is known from The Word that there was an influx from the world of spirits and from heaven into the prophets, partly by dreams, partly by visions, and partly by speech, and also with some into the very speech and into the very gestures, and thus into the things that belong to the body; and that at the time they did not speak from themselves, nor act from themselves, but from the spirits who were then in possession of their bodies. At such times some of them behaved like insane persons, as Saul did when he lay naked; others when they wounded themselves; others when they put horns on themselves, and others in similar ways. And as I desired to know in what manner these men were actuated by spirits, I was shown by means of a living experience. To this end I was for a whole night possessed by spirits, who took such possession of my body that I had only a very obscure sensation that it was my own body. AC 6212

In Swedenborg's terms the higher-order spirits would be angels who come to assist the person. As Swedenborg described it, they reside in the interior mind, which does not think in words but in universals that comprise many particulars (AC 5614).

The speech of the angels is also full of wisdom, because it proceeds from their interior thought; and their interior thought is wisdom, as their interior affection is love, their love and wisdom uniting in speech. Consequently it is so full of wisdom that they can express by one word what man cannot express by a thousand words. The ideas of their thought also comprehend things which man cannot conceive, much less utter. This is why the things which have been heard and seen in heaven are said to be ineffable, and such as ear hath not heard nor eye seen. It has been granted me to know by experience that it is so. I have sometimes been let into the state in which angels are, and in that state I have spoken with them; and then I understood all; but when I was brought back to my former state, and thus into the natural thought proper to man, and wished to recollect what I had heard, I could not; for there were thousands of things not adapted to the ideas of natural thought, thus not expressible at all by human words, but only by variegations of heavenly light. HH 239

But this is true not only in heaven but in the interior of mind too.

That man's interior mind . . . does not think from the words of any language, nor consequently from natural forms, can be seen by anyone who reflects on these things, for he can think in a moment what he can scarcely utter in an hour, and he does so by universals which comprise many particulars. These ideas are spiritual. AC 5614

The higher order in one patient showed him visually hundreds of universal symbols in the space of one hour. Though he found them entertaining he couldn't understand their meaning. One patient described a higher-order spirit who appeared all in white, radiant, very powerful in his presence, and who communicated directly with the spirit of the patient to guide him out of his hell. Swedenborg described how the influx of angels gently leads to good and leaves the person in freedom (AC 6205). I've described the incident where the patient recognized good forces first as a sun that withdrew from him when he was frightened whereas all his experiences of the lower order had been attacking ones. It was this simple respect for his freedom that led the patient to believe this was another order.

Swedenborg indicated that good spirits have some degree of control over the evil ones (AC 5992, 6308; SD 3525). Higher-order hallucinations have made the same comment —that they can control lower-order ones—but it is seldom to the degree the patient would desire. In some respects they overcome the evil insofar as the patient identifies with them. In one case I encouraged the patient to become acquainted with these helpful forces that tended to frighten him. When he did so their values merged into him, and the evil plotters, who had been saying for months they would kill him, disappeared. I seem to see some kind of control of the higher order over the lower, though the nature and conditions of this control are not yet clear. Again, and precisely in agreement with Swedenborg, I found evil spirits cannot see the good ones, but the good can the evil (HH 583). The lower order may know of the presence of the higher order but cannot see it.

Why the higher-order hallucinations were rarer remained

a considerable puzzle to me for over a year, since they were far more interesting to the patient and myself and potentially more therapeutic. Again, Swedenborg has an explanation that fits beautifully with my findings. I have noticed the higher order tends to be nonverbal and highly symbolic. He indicated that angels possess the very interior of man. Their influx is tacit. It does not stir up material ideas or memories but is directed to man's ends or inner motives (AC 5854, 6193, 6209). It is for this reason not so apparent and hence rarer in the patients' reports.

Conclusion

What are we to make of this similarity? I am personally convinced that Swedenborg and contemporary hallucinating persons are describing the same general experiences. There are just too many similarities to believe otherwise. Yet it is in itself remarkable that Swedenborg and persons separated by different cultures, different assumptions of the world, different experiences, and two centuries of time could so describe inner experiences alike. One implication is that this inner world may be very stable and consistent over centuries of time, certainly more consistent than the outer natural world.

Could Swedenborg have been mad? There is simply no evidence for this. In contrast to the limited, impaired, unproductive lives of these patients, his life was one of the richest and most productive ever lived. He explored voluntarily what patients are involuntarily thrown into.

None of these psychotics sought these experiences. They had all tried everything they could think of to stop the hallucinations—prayer, diet, obeying the voices, disregarding the voices, etc. Nothing worked. Even when extrasensory perception turned up it simply convinced them of the power of the "others" and frightened them. For every pleasant moment in this inner world, there was so much misery that most did not want to have these experiences. In contrast, Swedenborg sought to penetrate the inner world. He carefully recorded it and made great use of it.

It appears that psychotics, alienated from their own feelings and inner processes, find these processes represented around them in a different form. I'll illustrate by a humorous example. The same man who had a very gifted female spirit enlivening his life came in one day and complained of having female breasts. They got in the way of his work. He wasn't so crazy that he didn't know that others couldn't see the breasts. Yet he could, and it annoyed him. I asked him to describe the breasts. One side was well shaped, the other pendulous and not so attractive. I asked if he could associate with them. Yes. The well-shaped side reminded him of a new girl friend. The less attractive pendulous side reminded him of an old girl friend toward whom he still felt obligated. I said he should make up his mind between them. He did, and the breasts disappeared. Hallucinations were rarely this easily cured, but over and over I had the impression that they represented unknown potentials in the patient. The hell side illustrated personal faults, blindness and stupidity. The heaven side represented higher, unused gifts. There were no hallucinations at the patients' average level of functioning. They were either far more limited or more gifted than the patient. They appear to be unrealized, unlived-out potentials, spilling out to confuse the environment. A saintly lady patient had dirty voices. The drunken black burglar was shown a detailed and sensitive history of minority groups. In this sense, these people seemed to have too much unused, unrecognized, unconscious, which lived anyway and confused their environment. So my impressions conform to the general ideas of the unconscious.

Yet it is much more than that. There are demons that can

plague a person and try to possess him. There are also higher spirits whose wisdom is very great. In the head of the uneducated gas pipe fitter was the most gifted woman I've ever known. Quite to his surprise and faint amusement he found universal symbols all over the room. My guess is that the spiritual world is much as Swedenborg described it, and is the unconscious. We are mostly unconscious of the other spiritual worlds. It is meant to be that way, for it is very dangerous when these worlds are opened up to man, just as Swedenborg said. He did not advocate that anyone try to follow him.

My guess is that Swedenborg systematically explored the same worlds that psychotic patients find themselves thrust into, and these worlds are heaven and hell, the worlds beyond this one, inside this one. It is not too surprising, when you think of it, that persons who are disordered inwardly experience some of the raw underpinnings of experience that are invisible to the smoothly functioning mind.

To help us understand this phenomenon fully, let me describe what it would be like to be possessed in the normal sense. Swedenborg said that we all have spirits with us; they are part of the foundation and energy of mental processes. What would their presence be like in the normal mind that is not so alienated from its own nature, as in the patients' cases? Even though outwardly occupied in some normal train of thought and action, the lower order would appear as an impulse to think of some sexual, hostile, or other emotional scene. The impulse would feel like one's own, but arise contrary to what you thought you were choosing. In religious terms this is called temptation. At the point of choosing one line of experience and stumbling on another within, you feel that you can choose which one to dwell on. If you choose to put down the sexual, it could arise again and again, i.e., the temptation wouldn't disappear easily. And what would the interaction with angels be like? It could be finding yourself drifting into considering the quality of your conduct, or to understand your life or life itself in a broader way. This is the normal aspect of what the patients experienced in a more intense form. Most mental experience is participated in by spirits who don't know themselves as anything other than your own feelings. Honed down to this fine level, the only thing left that is really yours is the struggle to choose. Those who aren't choosing are going the way the spiritual winds blow. So the pitiful picture of the hallucinated psychotic is really an exaggerated picture of everyone's situation.

Minor Miracles

It is natural to look with some incredulity on Emanuel Swedenborg's claims. We would like some further confirmation that he really had reached other worlds. A number of incidents tend to provide such confirmation. In addition to everything else, Swedenborg had apparently stumbled upon a way to knowledge not often given to mortals. Yet he considered his new powers of so little account that he didn't even bother to mention them in his writings—even though he seemed to have recorded everything else. The confirmatory incidents I shall report here were all recorded out of the amazement of others.[25] Rather than let these somewhat miraculous incidents stand as evidence or proof that Swedenborg had indeed reached other worlds, I prefer to show them for their implications on the nature of reality and the inner nature of this man's personal experience. Proof for Swedenborg appropriately rested on how well what he had to say fit with human experience and biblical revelation. These are internal or spiritual evidences. These little miracles, though very curious, are not really proof of anything.

If Swedenborg had felt that a public display of his powers

would further the welfare of others, he probably would have displayed them widely. In several places he said that miracles have a coercive effect on belief and destroy the free will in spiritual matters (TCR 501, 849). Only choices made in freedom really affect the individual's eternal nature and destiny. Impressive, miraculous events tend to affect the externals of belief. In time the internal, freely chosen path comes to rule and even miraculous events are washed away in the current of time and forgotten. Indeed, one of the incidents is an example of this. Swedenborg accidentally showed his powers to John Wesley, the founder of Methodism. Wesley was very impressed for a while, but later joined others in rejecting Swedenborg. Miracles only impress when they demonstrate what are already the essentials of a person's beliefs. So Swedenborg mostly concealed his unusual powers; they were discovered by others almost by accident.

There were several clear indications that Swedenborg did not want to be an impressive public figure. His most valuable writings were issued anonymously until near the end of his life. (Only his printers knew their author.) Moreover, these sublime works were sold at less than the cost of printing (Docs II, p. 496). He lived a quiet, scholarly life, only going to the court or parties occasionally. He had a speech impediment and would often stammer so that the listener had to be patient and wait for the great man to get it out. Those who stammer are sensitive to the impact of social intercourse. The more tense and anxious the situation, the more they worry if they will stammer and the more they do. Swedenborg probably had a partial impediment that tended to disappear in relaxed company with friends. He never sought any public position other than his job as assessor of mines for Sweden. He had turned down a professorship. His whole adult life was to be spent in inner exploration and writing, which suited his nature, where he was comfortable. Left to his own devices, he was a quiet scholar in seedy clothes.

Further, when it became known that Swedenborg had unusual powers, an unpleasant flap was raised. There was much talk and rumor about what he had or hadn't done. Rumor serves the personal needs of those who carry it and an incident becomes distorted in the direction of these needs.

So Swedenborg had plenty of reason to play down these powers. Their use here is to show what is possible and to illustrate the inner experience of the expert on inner experience.

On July 17, 1759, Swedenborg and fifteen others were guests of the prominent merchant William Castel in Gothenberg at his fine home on Canal Street. At six in the evening Swedenborg appeared quite pale and alarmed. When asked what was wrong, he described a fire burning at that moment in Stockholm, three hundred miles away. He paced in and out of the house evidently agitated by the fire. His detailed description and evident sincerity upset the guests, many of whom were from Stockholm. Swedenborg described exactly where the fire was burning, where it had started, and when, and was dismayed to see a friend's house already in ashes. The next day, Sunday, the governor, having heard of the incident, asked to see Swedenborg and received a detailed report. The news spread through the city. Two days after the fire, messengers arrived and confirmed every detail as Swedenborg had reported it, including when and how it started, what it burned, and where and when it was contained (Docs II, pp. 628 f.). There were several separate reports of this incident that agreed on essentials. Even the German philosopher Immanuel Kant was impressed and sent his own agent to check the details.

This was the first incident. If it had not been for his evident alarm Swedenborg, now seventy-one, might have continued to conceal this extrasensory power. But the cat was out of the bag. Rumor started. A few began to suspect that he might even be the anonymous author of the extraordinary works on heaven and hell. People started asking questions about the spiritual world. He felt privileged to know so much and obliged to share it with others. He would answer simply and directly any questions, often referring to recent meetings with departed figures. People reacted as one might expect. Some were pleased to get such direct answers bearing on important matters. Others were surprised that this old man could look and act so sane and yet be so crazy. Evidently Swedenborg refused to check on departed friends just to satisfy curiosity. He said that this world and the spiritual world were separated for good reason. Apparently he would search in heaven or hell if the inquirer had a sufficiently weighty reason, as in the next two incidents.

In April or May 1761, a countesse de Marteville came to Swedenborg. Her husband, M. de Marteville, ambassador extraordinary of the Netherlands, had died in Sweden. He had given her a valuable silver service before he died. Now the silversmith was demanding a payment she could not afford even though she was sure her husband had paid for it. The matter was urgent to the woman. She had heard Swedenborg could contact the souls of the departed. Would he contact her husband and ask of the receipt? Swedenborg said he would. Three days later he returned and said he had spoken with her husband. The receipt was in a bureau upstairs. The woman said she had already searched the bureau. The husband had told Swedenborg that a certain drawer was to be pulled out and a false back removed. The woman and her company went upstairs and found the receipt and other lost papers as directed. This incident was related by eleven different sources, most of whom agreed on the above account (Docs II, pp. 633 f.). When questioned on the matter Swedenborg also affirmed its occurrence.

The next corroborated incident occurred several months later. Queen Louisa Ulrica of Sweden had heard of Swedenborg. She asked Count Scheffer about this man who pretended to talk with the dead. Was he perhaps mad? Count Scheffer knew Swedenborg and replied he was quite sane. He promised to bring him to court. Swedenborg went to court in his nobleman's finery, powdered wig and dress sword. After the queen chatted with foreign ambassadors and other dignitaries, Court Scheffer introduced Swedenborg to her. She asked whether he could really converse with the deceased? He answered yes. She asked if this skill could be learned by others. He said it couldn't, that it was a gift of the Lord. After some further conversation, the queen asked him to take a commission to her brother. The queen, the king, Count Scheffer, and Swedenborg adjourned to a quiet spot where the queen gave Swedenborg her message. The queen and her brother had been separated by tragedy because their countries were at war with each other when he died. Afterward they dined at the royal table, where Emanuel patiently answered many questions of the spiritual world. Many observers felt the queen had not really asked anything very serious of Swedenborg because she didn't really believe in his powers.

Some time afterward Count Scheffer again brought Swedenborg to court. He met the queen in her White Room surrounded by ladies-in-waiting. She lightly asked if he had a message from her brother. Swedenborg answered yes and suggested that they speak alone, and he related what he had learned from the queen's brother. The queen was variously described as in shock, disturbed, or so indisposed that she had to retire. She said later that Swedenborg had reported what no other living person knew. Swedenborg's servants reported that for days all the great people of the realm came in carriages to learn the queen's secret, but he did not reveal it (Docs II, pp. 647–666).

Later a reporter asked the queen of the incident and she affirmed it. The royal person was described as no weak-minded woman. "Nevertheless, she appeared to me so convinced of Swedenborg's supernatural intercourse with spirits, that I scarcely durst venture to intimate any doubts . . . and a royal air—'Je ne suis pas facilement dupée (I am not easily fooled), put an end to all my attempts at refutation" (Docs II, p. 649).

This particular incident was talked about the most, so there are more sources for it, including the queen herself. When Swedenborg was asked of the incident, he said it was true, "but he did not dwell upon [it] observing that there were hundreds of similar stories; but he did not think it worth while to waste many words upon them; saying that all these things were trifles . . . in the shade of the great object of his mission" (Docs II, p. 648). His mission was to bring to people the real nature of the spiritual and open up the meanings in the Bible. Alongside this, these were just curious stories.

The next story came from a Dr. Krohl who was reported to be a trustworthy gentleman. It fits with what is already known of Swedenborg. In the 1760s there was a very popular game of cards called Tresett.

One day a certain prelate, Archbishop Troilus, whose greatest pleasure consisted in playing the game of Tresett and who had lately lost one of his gambling friends, Erland Broman, met Swedenborg a short time after Broman's death in a large company, where he wished to amuse himself and the rest of the company at Swedenborg's expense. He asked him therefore in a jocular tone, "Bye the bye, assessor, tell us something about the spirit world. How does my friend Broman spend his time there?" Swedenborg answered instantly, "I saw him but a few hours ago shuffling his cards in the company of the evil one, and he was only waiting for your worship to make up a game of Tresett." The conversation between the archbishop and Swedenborg was thus brought to a close, and it is not difficult to see which of the two became the subject of the company's mirth. Docs III, p. 725

It apparently didn't pay to fool around with a man who had contact with heaven and hell! The archbishop was ultraorthodox and distinguished himself by the severe measures he undertook to suppress superstition (Docs III, p. 1246).

In the early 1800s an effort was made to collect anecdotes on Swedenborg. The next one was recounted by a Professor Scherer, professor of French at the University of Tübingen. Scherer was a French diplomat when he met Swedenborg. Though he witnessed the following incident, he did not believe in Swedenborg's spiritual powers.

The professor who was greatly advanced in years, then told us, that "in Stockholm, in all companies, very much was said concerning the spirit-seer Swedenborg, and wonderful things were recorded respecting his intercourse with spirits and angels. But the judgment pronounced concerning him was various. Some gave full credit to his visions; others passed them by as incomprehensible; and others rejected them as fanatical; but he himself [Scherer] had never been able to believe them. Swedenborg, however, on account of his excellent character, was universally held in high estimation."

Amongst other things Professor Scherer related the following remarkable occurrence: Swedenborg was one evening in company in Stockholm, when, after his information about the world of spirits had been heard with the greatest attention, they put him to the proof as to the credibility of his extraordinary spiritual communications. The test was this: He should state, which of the company would die first. Swedenborg did not refuse to answer this question, but after some time, in which he appeared to be in profound and silent meditation, he quite openly replied, 'Olof Olofsohn will die tomorrow morning at forty-five minutes past four o'clock.' By this predictive declaration, which was pronounced by Swedenborg with all confidence, the company were placed in anxious expectation, and a gentleman who was a friend of Olof Olofsohn, resolved to go on the following morning at the time mentioned by Swedenborg, to the house of Olofsohn, to see whether Swedenborg's prediction was fulfilled. On the way thither he met the well-known servant of Olofsohn, who told him that his master had just then died; a fit of apoplexy had seized him, and had suddenly put an end to his life. . . . The clock in Olofsohn's dwelling apartment stopped at the very minute in which he had expired, and the hand pointed to the time. Docs III, pp. 716–717

Emperor Peter III of Russia had fallen from power to be replaced by Empress Catherine, his wife. Peter was strangled ignominiously in a prison at Kopscha, Russia. At the same time Swedenborg was attending a party in Amsterdam. In the middle of a conversation he seemed to change radically. He was no longer aware of those around him. When he recovered, he was asked what had happened. At first he refused to tell it. After much coaxing he described in a somber and convincing manner the death of Peter III, asking that the partygoers note the date and his description so they might later compare it with the newspaper account. In a few days, the newspapers carried the story (Docs II, p. 490).

Christopher Springer was a noted Swedish politician and a old friend of Swedenborg's. Springer had been a major figure in some secret negotiations between Sweden and Prussia. Some years after Swedenborg's death he testified that the seer showed he knew precisely how the negotiations had taken place, who was present, what money was offered, etc., though they had been a closely guarded secret. Springer noted that he knew a great deal more besides. Springer was surprised that Swedenborg held him in such favor. It appeared to arise from the fact that Swedenborg knew not only what he did, but the good intentions behind Springer's diplomatic acts (Docs II, p. 533).

Swedenborg made many voyages by sailing ships. Voyaging in his time was a much more uncertain affair than it is now. Weather couldn't be predicted very well, a ship might or might not have a fast passage, and marine disaster was common enough. Swedenborg indicated that he did not fear a voyage, for he had angels with him. Somehow, moreover, when the enlightened Swedenborg was aboard, the vessel was likely to have an unusually swift passage. We cannot really determine whether or not this was mere chance. But at least he acquired a reputation that made sea captains happy to see him come aboard. Once a passenger expressed doubts about the odd Swedenborg who went into trances in his cabin. The captain was a more practical man. What Swedenborg did in his cabin was no matter to him; he paid his fare, was congenial, and brought a fair wind with him. This was sufficient for a practical-minded man.

There is a clear indication that at least on one occasion Swedenborg knew precisely when the vessel would conclude a long voyage under the uncertain influence of winds. The following incident was found in a letter from Christopher Springer, Swedenborg's friend, to Abbé Perrnety.

I will now relate to you some things which I have seen and heard. Fifteen years ago Swedenborg set out for Sweden and asked me to procure a good captain for him, which I did. I contracted with one whose name was Dixon. Swedenborg's luggage was taken on board the vessel; and as his apartments were at some distance from the docks, we engaged lodgings for the night in an inn near the harbour, as the captain above-named was to call for him in the morning. He went to bed, and I sat in another room with the landlord, with whom I conversed. We heard a noise; and not being able to tell the cause, we approached a door, which had a little window looking into the room where Swedenborg was sleeping. We saw him with his hands raised towards heaven, and his body apparently very much agitated. He spoke much for half-an-hour, but we could not understand what he was saying, except when he dropped his hands, when we heard him say with a loud voice, "My God!" but could not hear more. He remained very quietly in bed. I stepped into his room with the landlord, and asked whether he was ill. "No," said he, "but I have had a long discourse with the angels and the heavenly friends, and am at this time in a great perspiration." As his things had been taken on board, he asked the landlord for a fresh shirt and a fresh sheet. Afterwards he went to bed again, and slept till morning.

When the captain of the vessel called for Swedenborg, I took leave of him, and wished him a happy journey: having asked the captain, if he had a good supply of provisions on board, he answered me that he had as much as would be required. Swedenborg then observed, "My friend, we have not need of a great quantity; for this day week we shall, by the aid of God, enter into the port of Stockholm at two o'clock." On Captain Dixon's return, he related to me that this happened exactly as Swedenborg had foretold. Docs II, pp. 531 f.

Again Swedenborg showed he knew the future. The voyage from London to Stockholm had been made in a square-rigged ship. If you look at the map, it is not a straight simple journey but one with many changes of course over quite a distance. In a letter to a Dr. Beyer, Swedenborg described the voyage, "The trip from England was made in eight days; a favourable wind increasing to a perfect storm carried the ship along in style" (Docs II, p. 250). Of more interest is the description of Swedenborg in a trance. He talked unclearly and gestured visibly. It is also to be noted that when he came out of the trance he was perfectly oriented to this world. I cannot account for the heavy perspiration, but it has been observed by others in trance states. There is a legend that Buddha became very hot during his great vision under the Bodhi Tree. Nature came to help him: snails crawled over his head to cool him. In some representations of Buddha, many knobs on the head represent these snails.

An example of clairvoyance was given by Madame A. A. De Frese, wife of a Captain Carl George De Frese and granddaughter of the manufacturer Bolander of Gottenburg.

In a large company assembled in Gottenburg about 1770 in honour of Swedenborg, there was present the manufacturer Bolander, who was the owner of very extensive cloth-mills. During dinner Swedenborg suddenly turned to Mr. Bolander, and said to him sharply: "Sir, you had better go to your mills!" Mr. Bolander was very much surprised at the tone of voice in which Swedenborg spoke to him, and thought it anything but polite; but he rose nevertheless from the table, and went to his mills. On arriving there he found that a large piece of cloth had fallen down near the furnace, and had commenced burning. If he had delayed but a little longer, he would have found his property in ashes. After removing the danger, Mr. Bolander returned to the company and expressed his thanks to Swedenborg, telling him what had happened. Swedenborg smiled, and said that he had seen the danger, and also that there was no time to be lost, whereby he had addressed him thus abruptly. Docs III, p. 724

Two more examples cover the known little miracles that Swedenborg was involved in. There was a John Henry Jung, called Stilling, born in 1740. He was a self-made man, having risen from a tailor's apprentice to professor of political economy and later a privy councillor (Docs III, pp. 1163 f.). Jung-Stilling felt Swedenborg was possessed by spirits and that he ought to have resisted them. Swedenborg was well acquainted with the possibility of possession. He described himself as not possessed, but simply given the chance to explore the spiritual world. Jung-Stilling gave an account of another incident that would otherwise have been forgotten, vouching for it with the greatest certainty.

About the year 1770, there was a merchant in Elberfeld, with whom, during my seven years of my residence there, I lived in close intimacy. He was a strict mystic in the purest sense. He spoke little; but what he said, was like golden fruit on a salver of silver. He would not have dared, for all the world, knowingly to have told a falsehood. This friend of mine, who has long ago left this world for a better, related to me the following anecdote:

His business required him to take a journey to Amsterdam, where Swedenborg at that time resided; and having heard and read much of this singular man, he formed the intention of visiting him, and becoming better acquainted with him. He therefore called upon him, and found a very venerable-looking friendly old man, who received him politely, and requested him to be seated; on which the following conversation began:

Merchant. Having been called hither by business, I could not deny myself the honour, Sir, of paying my respects to you: Your writings have caused me to regard you as a very remarkable man.

Swedenborg. May I ask where you are from?

Merchant. I am from Elberfeld, in the duchy of Berg. Your writings contain so much that is beautiful and edifying, that they have made a deep impression upon me: but the source from whence you derive them is so extraordinary, so strange and uncommon, that you will perhaps not take it amiss of a sincere friend of truth, if he desires incontestable proofs that you really have intercourse with the spiritual world.

Swedenborg. It would be very unreasonable if I took it amiss; but I think I have given sufficient proofs, which cannot be contradicted.

Merchant. Are these the well-known ones, respecting the Queen, the fire in Stockholm, and the receipt?

Swedenborg. Yes, those are they, and they are true.

Merchant. And yet many objections are brought against them. Might I venture to propose, that you give me a similar proof?

Swedenborg. Why not? Most willingly!

Merchant. I had formerly a friend, who studied divinity at Duisberg, where he fell into consumption, of which he died. I visited this friend, a short time before his decease; we conversed together on an important topic: could you learn from him what was the subject of our discourse?

Swedenborg. We will see. What was the name of your friend?

The merchant told him his name.

Swedenborg. How long do you remain here?

Merchant. About eight or ten days.

Swedenborg. Call upon me again in a few days. I will see if I can find your friend.

The merchant took his leave and dispatched his business. Some days afterwards, he went again to Swedenborg, full of expectation. The old gentleman met him with a smile, and said, "I have spoken with your friend; the subject of your discourse was *the restitution of all things.*" He then related to the merchant, with the greatest precision, what he, and what his deceased friend had maintained.

My friend turned pale; for this proof was powerful and invincible. He inquired further, "How fares it with my friend: Is he in a state of blessedness?" Swedenborg answers, "No, he is not yet in heaven; he is still in Hades, and torments himself continually with the idea of the restitution of all things." This answer caused my friend the greatest astonishment. He exclaimed, "My God! What, in the other world?" Swedenborg replied, "Certainly; a man takes with him his favourite inclinations and opinions; and it is very difficult to be divested of them. We ought, therefore, to lay them aside here." My friend took his leave of this remarkable man, perfectly convinced, and returned back to Elberfeld. Docs II, pp. 487 f.

There is one more incident that almost lends a master touch to all the rest, but because it repeats the import already seen in these, I would like to pause to examine their implications. Though several incidents were viewed at the time to illustrate his spiritual powers, these seem to illustrate what is now called extrasensory perception (ESP). In three examples Swedenborg is with company and suddenly sees what is going on at a distance. These are the Stockholm fire, the death of Peter III, and the start of the factory fire. These were all matters that touched on his life. The Stockholm fire was burning toward his property; the fire in the factory was about to wipe out a friend. It is not as clear that he was emotionally involved in the death of Peter. My guess is that he was. He was a nobleman who voted in the House of Lords. He was concerned with European wars and treaties as illustrated by his intimate knowledge of the negotiations between Sweden and Prussia. It appears that important information concerning present events could break in on his awareness. This is clairvoyance. Since these events are two centuries old there could have been many more examples of the same phenomena that were not recorded.

Two incidents suggest that Swedenborg had precognition: his predictions of the death of Olof Olofsohn and when his sea voyage would end. In the Olofsohn case he apparently sought the information and got it at will. The last incident to be reported also involves precognition.

Three events appear to involve searching out and communicating with someone who has died. These are the incident with the queen, finding the lost receipt, and contacting a friend for the merchant. Though the queen said that Swedenborg had reported what no living person knew, actually she knew, or she couldn't have affirmed it. Contacting the friend for the merchant was similar. Conceivably Swedenborg could have read the queen's and the merchant's minds. The incident of the lost receipt is another matter, for there was no one around whose mind could be read. It had to have been a matter of postcognition (reading the past husband's mind, that no longer existed on earth) or directly contacting the husband who still existed in some other realm.

Apparently this information was available at will; Swedenborg just needed a little time to seek it out. Also, not all information was spontaneously given to him. For instance, his sister had died and he did not know of it (Docs II, p. 559). When chided about this he said, in effect, that he hadn't asked about her. Also, he was emotionally distant from her at the time. He could find out what he wanted of the past, present, or future, and present information would break in on his awareness if it concerned him. Here was a gift many want to have and many would try to use to their profit. What one could do with a few days foreknowledge of the stock market, for instance! Yet Swedenborg considered his gift of remarkably little importance.

Underlying this lies the more fundamental question of the relationship of ESP powers and this realm? There was little in Swedenborg's writings to suggest a connection between them. We have thought of ESP and being a spirit seer as separate phenomena, but I believe they arise from the same source, and if they are not identical, they are close enough that it should be no surprise that they arise together.

First let us look at the matter from Swedenborg's view-point. He had angels from heaven and spirits from hell with him all the time. He said clearly that everyone does. His advantage was that he could see and talk with them. Also, he was so familiar with the spiritual worlds that he could distinguish between those from hell and those from heaven. Spirits from hell often claimed they could predict the future, but they really couldn't. This is true, too, when dealing with contemporary lower-order hallucinations. They like to pretend that they predict and even control the future, but this doesn't hold up under even a simple test.

The matter is quite the opposite in heaven. The Lord knows the whole of existence—past, present, or future. The Lord, heaven, and angels essentially transcend time. From this, it is possible for anyone in contact with angels to do all that Swedenborg did—read the past, present, or future or contact those who had died. What we see as foresight here is actually a part of divine providence.

From this we can see how greatly the man errs who believes that the Lord has not foreseen, and does not see, the minutest things appertaining to man, and that in these he does not foresee and lead; when the truth is that the Lord's foresight and providence are in the very least of these minutest things connected with man, in things so very minute that it is impossible by any thought to comprehend as much as one out of a hundred millions of them; for every smallest moment of man's life involves a series of consequences extending to eternity, each moment being as a new beginning to those which follow; and so with all and each of the moments of his life; both of his understanding and of his will. And as the Lord foresaw from eternity what would be man's quality, and what it would be to eternity, it is evident His providence is in the minutest things, and . . . governs and bends man to such a quality; and this by a continual moderating of his freedom. AC 3854

An analogy can be used to illustrate this time situation. A road winds a long way up a mountain. The driver on the road sees just the little stretch that involves him. Someone at the top of the mountain can look down on all the drivers and predict when and where one coming down would meet a driver coming up. Heaven, at the top of the mountain, looks down on our limited conception of time. Anyone in contact with heaven can get this kind of information. The real issue is not whether it happens, but under what circumstances and to what purpose. The circumstances refer back to the whole matter of the way Swedenborg entered this inner state and what he was inwardly. He even indicated that his actual way of breathing had to change before he could perceive heaven. I think that the boundary between our wanting to know the future and the higher knowledge of the spiritual world is just about where Swedenborg placed it. These worlds were meant to be separate. Only for good purposes and only rarely could the knowledge of one show in the other.

Look again at the incidents. At the time of the Stockholm fire, Swedenborg was still resolved to conceal that he had this added knowledge. The whole experience of seeing and reporting the fire happened against his will. Its good effect was to thrust him out of hiding. Today, this is the incident most often associated with the mystic from Sweden. Once his gift had been revealed, Swedenborg used it mostly for the good of others—though he considered it very unimportant. The incidents with the queen, Olof Olofsohn, Peter III, the voyage, and contacting the merchant's friend stimulated some to consider his works and a few to believe him. The incident of the receipt saved a good woman from financial distress. The incident of the factory fire saved a friend from loss. Apparently many people asked Swedenborg to check up on deceased friends and he refused, because the good served was not sufficient. In many places Swedenborg describes the Lord or heaven as good itself. It is curious that heaven answers insofar as good is served.

Though most of the incidents involve ESP, some involve

the apparent contact with a person's spirit. I think these are part of the same phenomena, contact with a realm whose time system transcends ours. Swedenborg casually mentions that angels lose the sense of what men on earth mean by time, for their time is inward, as change of state. What does daybreak mean to an angel? Why, the dawning of understanding, of course! What else could it mean?

This last incident always seems somewhat humorous to me. Unlike many contemporary mystics, gurus, and occultists, Swedenborg didn't mean to show his powers. Yet, he again stumbled into doing so by accident. This incident is well attested to, since it involved John Wesley, the founder of Methodism.

The scene was a drawing room in England, February 1772. John Wesley was preparing for a religious speaking tour and the Reverend Samuel Smith and others were assisting him. The gathering was interrupted by the arrival of a letter that Wesley opened and read with evident astonishment.

> Great Bath Street
> Coldbath Fields
> February 1772
>
> Sir,
> I have been informed in the world of spirits that you have a strong desire to converse with me; I shall be happy to see you if you will favour me with a visit.
> I am, sir, your humble servant,
> Emanuel Swedenborg
> (Docs II, p. 565)

Wesley told these gentlemen that he did want to see Swedenborg but he had told no one of it. He answered Swedenborg, saying that their meeting would have to take place in six months, after his tour. Swedenborg wrote back that he could not meet him at that time, for he was to die on the twenty-ninth of the next month, which, of course, he did (Docs II, pp. 564 f.). Wesley was at first quite impressed, but when his follower Reverend Smith studied and took up Swedenborg's teachings, Wesley joined with those who held him mad.

At his death, Swedenborg was living with the barber Shearsmith and his family on Bath Street, London. At first the family was a little frightened of this great man who appeared to go into trances and held conversations in strange tongues with invisible strangers, but he came to be known and liked. They said he often went out in an old-fashioned suit of black velvet with long ruffles, a curious hilted sword, and a gold-headed cane. He ate little meat, concentrating on cakes, tea, sweetened coffee, and water. He used a great deal of snuff and fortunately spilled enough on his manuscripts to help preserve them from insects.

Toward the end he lay for some weeks in a trance without sustenance. Shortly before his death he suffered a stroke and partial paralysis on one side of his body. Friends brought him a Swedish minister named Ferelius, to give him the last rites. The minister spoke:

I observed to him, that, as quite a number of people thought his sole purpose in promulgating his new theological system had been to make himself a name, or to acquire celebrity, which object, indeed he had thereby attained, if such had been the case, he ought now to do the world the justice to retract it either in whole or part, especially as he could not expect to derive any additional advantage from this world, which he would soon leave. He thereupon half rose in his bed, and laying his sound hand upon his breast said with some manifestation of zeal: "As true as you see me before your eyes, so true is everything that I have written; and I could have said more, had it been permitted. When you enter eternity, you will see everything, and then you and I shall have much to talk about." Docs II, pp. 557–558

The minister didn't seem to really know Swedenborg. The old man gave the minister one of the few unsold copies of the

Arcana Coelestia. Since these twelve volumes are his most profound writings, it is unlikely the minister read much of them. Afterward the Shearsmiths' maid innocently commented that he had told them all of his death a few days before. She said he seemed pleased, "as if he was going to have a holiday, to go to some merry-making" (Docs II, p. 546), which may well have been the case. The man who knew what it was all about had no fear of dying.

8

Existence Itself as Symbolic

There is another fundamental indication that Swedenborg had indeed known higher worlds. His view of this world had completely turned around. Before 1745 he was very much embedded in the material world. In 1745, while exploring inward, he had difficulty understanding the strange symbolism and vagaries of inner processes. Yet within a few years he stood solidly in the feelingful world of heaven, ruled by One God. From this world all the lesser material worlds of man, of things, of the earth, had become symbolic. All existence had become an indication of the work of the Lord. He found meanings everywhere that only a few had suspected. And with this new understanding came the most difficult to understand and incredible aspect of Swedenborg. The description of heaven and hell might be accepted, but how was man to understand and accept that he himself, and all existence, are really just representations of the One?

What had happened was that Swedenborg then saw everything in relation to the Divine. What was creating existence, making things every moment to be as it was, had come into the first place. What was first in creation was first in his understanding. Everything else fell into secondary places as correspondents. All levels of existence were symbolic representations of the nature of the Divine. He must have experienced something fundamentally different to have shifted to such an awesome view of creation. The implications of this shift will be treated in a number of different ways so its sweeping implications will gradually become clearer.

All the orders of existence are steps down from the One which is the All. The One (called by a multitude of names in all times and cultures) is the Only and Self-subsistent. All other orders of existence are dependent both for their very nature and their continued existence. This stepping down into more and more limited orders of existence permits the One to be manifest on all possible levels, revealing its nature through all possible limitations.

Now, since all things in general and particular subsist from the Divine, that is, continually exist, and all things in general and particular which are therefrom cannot be otherwise than representative of those things whereby they came into existence, it follows, that the visible universe is nothing else than a theatre representative of the Lord's kingdom, and [this kingdom] is a theatre representative of the Lord Himself. AC 3483

The first step down is the celestial heaven, which in its celestial love corresponds most closely to the One Itself. The spiritual heaven is the next step down, a lesser representation, corresponding to celestial love, the love of one person for another (where "the joy of one is the joy of all"). The natural heaven is the lowest level of heaven. The world of spirits is the next level. Here men are opened to and discover their inner nature. And the world of spirits interacts with the inner processes of mind. Man's mind itself is a series of levels corresponding to all levels of the spiritual world, ranging from almost pure feelings to thoughts and ideas, to speech and gestures, to the body itself. Beyond man, animals, plants, and the physical world are further lower-order correspondents to the One. This whole series of existences corresponds to the One God who is thereby everywhere manifest. Not only man is made in the image, but creation itself is a series of images.

We can break into this series at any point and try to understand the nature of what is being represented. We can look at events in the world of spirits and see echoed there the general nature of heaven. Or we can look at a man's face and gestures and try to see what is being represented of his nature. Or we can look at animals and nature and try to see what is being represented of man's nature. This seems like an odd thing to do, but many of the occult sciences delve into precisely this kind of relationship. Any aspect of nature can be looked at as representing man, or the inner of man looked at as a representation of the spiritual world, or levels of heaven can be looked at to better understand God. God is not simply boss of the whole of existence. Of much more importance, the One is the most fundamental tendency, drift, or nature of existence. By seeing everything as symbolic or as correspondent, Swedenborg was looking at this drift of the real nature of things. Whether one believes it or not, cares or not, the drift is there anyway. He is seeing the source out of which things come and how they reflect that source. The end they serve reflects that source. It is very much as though Swedenborg came to see the real ends of existence. When asked why there is man at all, Swedenborg answered, that there may be a heaven. Man's life on earth is a seminary (seed bed, related to semen) for heaven.

This stepping down, imaging of existence, Swedenborg treated under the ideas of correspondence and representation. A priest, minister, or rabbi represents the holy of the Divine by his vestments and the services he conducts. This is true even if the man is quite evil. Swedenborg even says that because he represents this, the office and ceremony are to be respected even in the hands of an evil man. Where the representation is a good fit to what it represents, then it may be said to correspond. All existence *represents* God, but unless a thing has goodness in it, it doesn't *correspond* to God. A correspondent is then inwardly suitable. Correspondence is an organic relationship, just as an effect corresponds to its cause. Symbols are a more limited idea than what Swedenborg is dealing with. A symbol is often an image of something greater than itself. Swedenborg is dealing with existence itself, which is a larger idea than an image. All but God himself are representations or images.

Representations are nothing but images of spiritual things in natural ones, and when the former are rightly represented in the latter, then the two correspond. Yet the man who knows not what the Spiritual is, but only the Natural, is capable of thinking that such representations . . . are impossible, for he might say to himself, How can what is spiritual act upon what is material? But if he will reflect upon the things taking place in himself every moment, he may be able to gain some idea of these matters; for instance, how the will can act upon the muscles of the body, and effect real actions; also how thought can act upon the organs of speech . . . and also how the affections can act on the face, and there present images of themselves, so that another often thereby knows what is being thought and felt. These examples may give some idea of what representations and correspondences are. As such things are now presented in man, and as there is nothing that can subsist from itself, but only from some other, and this again from some other, and finally from the First, and this by a connection of correspondences, those who enjoy any extension of judgement may draw the conclusion that there is a correspondence between man and heaven; and further, between heaven and the Lord who is the First. AC 4044

Man's own functioning is one of the most concrete and immediate examples of correspondence. Our lives are a bridge between the spiritual within and the material without.

Our movements, gestures, speech, etc., correspond to the inner life. Inwardly we participate in a spiritual world. Outwardly, in our bodies, we are in the world of things.

The whole natural world corresponds to the spiritual world, not only the natural world in general, but also in particular. Whatever, therefore, in the natural world exists from the spiritual, is said to be its correspondent. By the natural world is meant whatever is under the sun. . . . But the spiritual world is heaven, and the things belonging to that world. . . . Since man is a heaven, and also a world, in least form after the image of the greatest, therefore in him there is a spiritual world and a natural world. The interiors, which belong to his mind, and relate to the understanding and will, make his spiritual world; but the exteriors, which belong to his body, and relate to its senses and actions, make his natural world. Whatsoever, therefore, in this natural world, that is, in his body, its senses and actions, exists from its spiritual world, that is, from his mind and its understanding and will, is called a correspondent. HH 89, 90

Parallels to Correspondence

At first Swedenborg's idea of correspondence may seem to be just an odd notion that creates a lot of symbolic understandings. It so pervades his writings that unless its sweep and importance is understood his writings seem odd. What does it mean that a particular group of people are located in heaven under the foot of the Grand Man? Why, it means they are particularly materialistic in their orientation. And the Grand Man? It's the full nature of humanness in heaven, *of which we are images.*

Swedenborg's idea of correspondences is the most general statement of an idea that has repeatedly turned up in the world's literature. It is both an ancient and modern idea, with so many parallels that it is not possible even to catalog them all.

Swedenborg often referred to correspondence as an ancient science that was later mostly lost.

That all things in nature, both in general and in particular, and also all things in the human body, correspond to spiritual things is shown in the work *Heaven and Hell.* What correspondence is, however, has hitherto been unknown; yet in most ancient times it was very well known, for to those who lived then the science of correspondence was the science of sciences, and was so universal that all their treatises and books were written by correspondences. The Book of Job, a book of the Ancient Church, is full of correspondences. The hieroglyphics of the Egyptians and the myths of antiquity were of a like nature. All the ancient churches were representative of spiritual things; the ceremonies and also the statues on which their worship was founded, consisted of pure correspondences. Of a like nature were all things of the church established among the children of Israel; their burnt offerings, their sacrifices, their meat-offerings, and their drink-offerings, with all things connected with them, were correspondences. So also was the tabernacle . . . their feasts . . . and their holy garments. TCR 201

I have been informed that the men of the most ancient church, which existed before the flood, were men of so heavenly a genius that they conversed with the angels of heaven; and that they had the power to do so by correspondences. Consequently their wisdom became such that, whatever they saw on earth, they thought of not only naturally, but also spiritually, thus also in conjunction with the angels of heaven. I was further informed that Enoch, who is mentioned in Genesis v. 21–24, and his associates, collected correspondences . . . and transmitted their knowledge to posterity. As a result of this the science of correspondences was . . . cultivated in many kingdoms in Asia, particularly in the Land of Canaan, Egypt, Assyria, Chaldaea, Syria, Arabia, and in Tyre, Sidan, and Nineveh. It was thence communicated to Greece; but it was there changed into fable. TCR 202

The ancients who had a knowledge of correspondences made for themselves images corresponding to heavenly things, and they took delight in them because they signified things of heaven and the church. These images therefore they set up, not only in their temples but also in their homes, not to worship them, but that they might remind them of the heavenly things which they signified. Thus in Egypt and elsewhere they set up in effigy calves, oxen, serpents, also children, old men and virgins; because calves and oxen signified the affections and powers of the natural man; serpents, the prudence and also the cunning of the sensual man; children, innocense and charity; old men, wisdom; and virgins, the affections . . . and so on. When, however, the knowledge of correspondences was lost, their posterity began to worship as holy, and at length as deities, the images and likenesses set up by the ancients, because they were in and about their temples. For the same reason the ancients worshipped in gardens and groves, according to the different kinds of trees growing in them, and also on mountains and hills. TCR 205

It would be possible to cull from Swedenborg's works a great deal of ancient, lost knowledge that he learned by conversing with these people in heaven. The result would give richness to ancient images and ceremonies that we are inclined to see as simple and primitive.

We have mostly lost the sense of this ancient language. Primitives who sat before a fire at night could read in the flames guidance as to how they should live. The flames corresponded to their will and understanding. With our present sophistication, we would say they were merely projecting their ideas into the forms of the flames. Swedenborg would not entirely disagree with this. Insofar as they projected from the deepest levels of themselves, they would be letting the spiritual world within show in the forms of the flames. This primitive animism still exists. In various parts of the world primitives consult trees, streams, rocks, and the sky, and they learn from and are guided by them. Swedenborg clearly compliments these primitives, for they were in easy communication with the spiritual world. Swedenborg's *Arcana Coelestia* and *Apocalypse Explained* say much about how

subsequent generations lost this primitive language of correspondence. The living, delicate experience of Jesus, about to
die, breaking bread with friends, becomes frozen into neat
little wafers. Worse yet, much of the inner life and meaning
goes out of ceremonies. Swedenborg dealt at length with the
meanings in the Jewish tabernacle, meanings that very few
practicing Jews even suspect (AC 9455 f.). Ceremony is a
partly alive, mostly dead, leftover of the primitive experience
of a correspondence between spiritual meaning and things in
the world.

There are many other former uses of correspondence. Ancient man gradually worked out a relationship of the configu-
ration of planets at birth and thereafter to an individual's
personality and contemporary problems. Astrology is an example of correspondence between the inner man and plan-
etary configurations. Though to many it seems a specious
science (as is true of all claimed correspondences), at least
Jung felt it had real merit.[26] The ancients had a whole host
of ways of trying to divine the future and find guidance by
the arrangement of material things, the fall of cards (Tarot),
tea leaves, yarrow sticks (I Ching), cracked bones (scalpula-
mancy), etc. Usually these systems required a considerable
amount of interpretation that allowed some projection of
inner processes. They didn't give simple yes or no answers.
Though at first this seems like a weakness, it is probably
critical to the effective functioning of these systems. If you
consult the I Ching or the Tarot asking a simple "shall I or
shan't I?" you are likely to get so rich an answer that it
requires your thinking deeper on the question and your purposes. Like the tremulous rapid movement of the flame, there
is room for the inner depths to be projected. Jung felt there
was actual synchronicity. The person who sincerely asked a
question of the fall of yarrow sticks (cards, coins, tea leaves,
etc.) found they fell into a pattern that was an image or
correspondent of deep inner processes. It may well be a

matter that believers find is true and nonbelievers find false because each one finds what reflects him!

Magic, in its deeper, older sense, is another example of correspondence. We think of magic mostly as the tricky sleight of hand of a showman. In its ancient sense the correspondence between the inner and outer was used to control the inner. For instance, if one believed that to stand in a ritualistically laid rope circle protected one from spiritual harm, it probably did. The outer rope circle, ceremoniously laid, corresponded symbolically to spiritual protection. This kind of magic including brewing every possible concoction (such as lizards' tails, gathered in the full of the moon!) and every kind of ceremony put to both good and evil uses. In voodoo practices we see contemporary examples of this. Believers make a statue of an enemy and put a pin in it to wound him. The statue and the pin wound correspond to the enemy and what one wants to happen to him. Although I don't believe Swedenborg commented directly on this use of correspondence, it appears his writing would not support its effectiveness. He always saw the real ruling force as inner. The outer only reflected it. Hence, if you believed the rope circle really worked, if it reflected your inner, it would be effective. But the voodoo doll could not hurt *me,* unless *I* really believed in its effectiveness. We have to say that this whole realm of correspondential magic is foolish or real, depending on your felt beliefs.

Swedenborg did comment that there were whole languages, such as the ancient Egyptian, that were based on spiritual correspondences. I believe all these languages began with pictures of animals and objects that were broadly symbolic and quite meaningful when coined. Or languages began by the correspondence between feeling and sound. Later generations only penetrated the outer shell of these languages, having lost the spirit of awe that went into their creation.

Ancient myth and religion were often heady brews of

correspondences to man's innermost experiences. Greek mythology is a good example (AC 2762). In later generations we again have lost the tremulous spirit that coined these myths, and what is left is just a collection of quaint stories.

Another example of correspondences is in ancient alchemy. When man knew little of chemicals and the magic of their chemistry, he could get very involved in the processes. Again, Jung penetrated the strange business of alchemistry to find medieval man attempting to reach spiritual integration (the philosopher's gold) in the midst of his strange brews. Jung did a most careful and well-illustrated description of this process. The chemical and inner processes corresponded. These deeply involved chemists were working at themselves in their retorts. It wasn't just a simple matter of putting things together in the right order. A woman, sex, religious symbols, meditation, great soul-searching and doubt were all involved. We now know too much to get so involved in chemistry. Or, one could say that we are too distant to get so involved.

Most of the examples of the use of correspondence come from ancient times. In many ways we are less capable of participating in this strange bridging of the inner and outer. Yet we can give modern examples of essentially the same process. The projective tests used by psychologists are a good example. Give a client some vague material and encourage him to shape the situation to suit him. He may be asked to tell what he sees in inkblots (Rorschach test), to draw a person (Machover test) or a tree, or to select a dramatic backdrop and cardboard figures and make a drama (MAPS test), or simply to copy geometric figures (Bender-Gestalt test).[27] Through long observation and study psychologists can read the personality traits of their clients from these creations. The client projects both what is conscious and unconscious. What he sees, how he reacts, or how he draws a simple line reflects his real personality. The way a person sees an inkblot corresponds to what he is. There isn't any particular magic in the test materials. To create a really simple test I once had people just make a dot on a page, but I abandoned it after distinguishing the brain-damaged, compulsive, neurotic, hostile, etc.

Another example of correspondence is in psychosomatic medicine. Some very real physical disorders are also representations of psychic conflict. The duodenal ulcer, for instance, often occurs in a person who denies dependency, and fights for self-sufficiency. But the poor stomach tells an opposite story. It says, feed me, take care of me. The stomach represents the unconscious need for dependency. Although migraine is partly hereditary and partly metabolic, it also represents a psychic situation. Very often the migraine person is unusually conscientious, self-driven, compulsive. The headache explodes and says, forget it all, you've forgotten yourself. Stop, rest, take care of yourself. Psychosomatic medicine is still a young branch of medicine, and it is not yet known if all disorders have this psychic component.[28]

This spontaneous natural language of the body was outlined by Swedenborg two centuries ago. It is not fair to say simply that Swedenborg founded psychosomatic medicine. What he was doing with the correspondences of the body and contemporary psychosomatic medicine are quite different. This medicine unwraps what diseased and distressed organs say psychologically; Swedenborg was dealing with normal organs. Yet there is a similarity. Swedenborg stressed that the heart and vascular system correspond to love. Psychosomatic disorders of the heart often have to do with strong feelings. He was not far off.[29]

Everyone's mind has a natural capacity to speak in the language of correspondences. This is probably why an understanding of this language has appeared in many different cultures at different times. Dreams are natural spontaneous phenomena showing the language of correspondence. Everyone dreams several times a night. There is good experimental evidence, now, that dreaming is a necessary process.[30] In dreams the inner potential of the individual images forth the situation of the dreamer. The dream uses imagery to dramatically represent the dreamer's situation. The correspondential language of dreams transcends our ordinary understanding, so we must learn to read this spontaneous internal language.

Closer to consciousness, there are many ways of meditating or allowing fantasy expression that again are natural examples of the language of symbolic representations. For instance, I have often taught groups to relaxedly gaze at anything in the room that catches their eye—patterns in the rug, cracks in the floor, a bit of rumpled paper, anything. With relaxed observation, what is looked at soon begins to suggest meanings. I recall one alcoholic woman who studied a crack in the floor. She tearfully saw in it the varied ups and downs of her life. We can at any time discover this inner representation of ourselves. We tend to represent ourselves even when we don't want to, when we form opinions of situations. The meanings we project into or find in situations very much reflect ourselves. The primitive studying the flames of a campfire and our projecting meaning into situations are really the same process except the primitive is a little more advanced. His is a more delicate and sensitive searching for meaning. Our opinions are a more abrupt categorizing of things.

In *The Natural Depth in Man*,[31] I describe a graduated series of inner states. The general tenor of these states, as we wander down the corridor of mind, is toward symbolization or representation. Whatever we are has a profound inner drift toward representing its real nature. Self-reflection, fantasy, visions, hallucinations, dreams—all are various levels of this single central tendency. I personally am convinced that this capacity to represent our real selves is the most primal and fundamental tendency in man. Even lowering the person slowly toward physical death via anesthesia, as my own experience has shown, greatly intensifies this process. This process exists in everyone, whether the individual believes it or not, cares or not, is educated or religious or not. It is a primal root tendency in humanness, and could well exist in the rest of the animal kingdom, since animals also seem to dream.

Rather than try to prove this tendency here (as I did in *The Natural Depth in Man*), it is more important to inquire why. What is the implication of this universal inborn disposition toward representing our inner selves? In my earlier work I systematically tried to nail down what we could infer of the source of this tendency. One main implication is that our minds or lives are designed with a kind of self-corrective, more-brilliant-than-us, internal guidance system. The main difficulty with this innate drift of wisdom is that its mode of thinking and understanding is higher than ours. Hence it reveals itself in a language of symbols that transcends our understanding. We have to learn to come up to it, to understand its wisdom. The main purpose of this internal system is that it sees, reflects, and comments on the quality of our life. It is apparently concerned with the inner nature and quality of each one's existence. It appears to operate from a plane in which all things are seen as related, from omniscience. This omniscient aspect is what causes it to be naturally and profoundly symbolic. The symbol arises in a sphere in which the nature of a thing is profoundly understood and seen in its relationship to everything else. Hence, in going within, Swedenborg worked through a forest of symbolism to arrive at the source of this process, the Divine itself.

Swedenborg says that the science of correspondences is the primary science of the ancients. With this brief sketch of just a few of the areas it involves, we can still agree it is a primary field of knowledge. Under the general heading of correspondences Swedenborg is dealing with the basic understanding involved in animism, divination, the formation of language, religious ceremony, astrology, magic, myth, alchemistry, projective tests, psychosomatic medicine, dream interpretation, interpreting fantasy, visions and hallucinations, and the like. Yet, to Swedenborg, these were relatively minor uses of correspondence. As we shall see later, he felt the greatest use was in unlocking the secrets of heaven hidden within the Bible.

The Language of Correspondence

There are several ways of learning the language of correspondence. Swedenborg began with the simplest one—the one that anyone can use—when he started working out the symbols that appeared in his dreams and hypnogogic experiences. The real advantage of the hypnogogic process is that one can experience a particular state and discover immediately how it is symbolized by the hypnogogic.

Another way to learn of it is direct revelation from heaven. After he was elevated to heaven Swedenborg read the Bible and found inner meanings opened to him.

There is a kind of sense to the language of correspondences or symbols. The inner uses real events of the world, showing great regard for the way man experiences things. The earth has the implications for most people of solid, safe, real, material in contrast to what is high, airy, less certain. Each symbol can be taken negatively or positively. Earth can mean safe, or solid. In the opposite sense it can mean earthbound, or limited. Each of these meanings is in relation to man's experience, and as such they correspond to aspects of man. We speak of a man as earthy. Again it can be taken two ways: as down to earth, in contrast to airy or flighty; or as limited, as though a clod (of earth).

Take the concept of hand. How do we experience our

hands? As we reach out and do something our power comes into use. Hand signifies power. A handmaid is one who assists my powers. A handyman has a general ability to do things. Swedenborg says the hand signifies power, the hand and arm greater power, and the shoulder, all power (AC 1085). A man who lent us his hands, arms, and shoulders would be pretty much doing his utmost for us.

My point is that the language of correspondence or symbols is intimately linked to the way people experience things. There are further clues in the slang use of words, such as lend a hand, bear a hand, hands down (they can't carry anything in that position), handy, and so forth. Where we have considerable experience of a thing, it is easier to recover these ancient meanings. Sight has to do with understanding, like "oh, I see." Hearing has to do with being receptive, i.e., "listen to me," or make yourself receptive to me.

There are also many symbols whose inner quality of meaning has been lost. For instance, bones have to do with the central nature of a man. The bone structure or innermost nature allows a man to stand up or reveal himself. Hence the old expression "he is bone of my bone," i.e., fundamentally like me. The kidney separates the unwanted waste material from the blood. The inner meaning is just that: what separates the unwanted from the wanted. The heart and blood vessel system is the warm red life within the person. There are many literary references to spilling of blood, meaning that life is escaping and being lost. The heart has a long association with life and love. The blood system is the inner, affective, feeling life of the individual. The lungs relate to both the inside and outside. They take in air from the outside and nourish the blood. What bridges the world outside and the life within is the understanding. The lungs and the whole respiratory system represent the understanding. Swedenborg says that in the spiritual world a man's faith or reception of truth may be perceived by the respiration of his lungs and the quality of his charity by the pulsation of his heart (DF 19). Here the symbolism is a little beyond what we can recognize easily. With a little loosening up of feeling and associations we can begin to read this language of correspondences. It is very like poetry. It is like moving into a new sphere of thought, because it opens up the interior of human experience and puts one at the threshold of spiritual thought.

We can begin to see how aspects of our own body represent aspects of our inner spiritual life. Sight is like seeing, i.e., understanding. Hearing is like making one's self receptive. But how can the outer world also be images of man, and ultimately of the spiritual world and God's nature? The Chinese see bamboo as like a gentleman. Look at the way it grows. It stands straight; it does not intrude on its neighbor. Here is an analogy. Swedenborg was speaking even more basically. In heaven the animals, plants, landscape literally represent the nature of the people there. Those in hell feel they are in pretty places, but seen in the light of heaven or truth their places look like small, dark, mean holes. Those who are spiritually rich find themselves in magnificent palaces with great gardens. In a subtle way this is true of us, too. The world we perceive reflects us. The holy man sees holy, sacred things; the businessman sees goods of such and such value.

An example using animals shows how Swedenborg saw existence as corresponding to man. We take animals to be real creatures occupying this world in ways similar to us. Animals really exist. Yet they also represent the possibilities of human feeling. For instance, the domestic cat has a clear affective disposition. It is soft, quiet, very oriented to its own comfort. It is like a particular kind of sensual pleasure. It is loyal as long as it is satisfied. Unsatisfied, it is likely to show its discontent and make demands to be fed or attended to. It represents this set of affective possibilities. Each individual cat differs to a degree, but these are its norms. It is like a theme and variation in music: the basic disposition of the domestic cat is the theme and individual cats are the variation. Cats exist in heaven. There they represent the affective orientation described above. Almost any observer of domestic cats will recognize this sensuous orientation. We sense it because we feel it in ourselves and empathize with it. This does not deny that there are real cats in the real world out there. This view goes beyond that, asking almost why cats at all. Beyond the real cat are the affective tendencies we can recognize, because it is like an aspect of ourselves; it goes beyond man to the possibilities in existence. In heaven there are no material things. There cats even more clearly represent an aspect of the inner life of angels that in turn reflect an aspect of the inner life of God. When Swedenborg spoke of representations or correspondents he was not in the least denying or overlooking the real, material world. He was looking through it to the whole of creation. That is how fundamental a shift the whole business of correspondence, or symbolic language, is.

Even if we aren't interested in how things are represented in the spiritual world, it still helps to see animals as corresponding to affections. The one who can feel in himself the disposition represented by a cat can deal with cats in an empathetic way, can please them. The gentle touch around the head makes the cat feel more comfortable and at home. The one who can understand the interactive parallels of cats and owners can appreciate the owner better through the cat. But if one wants to understand more than this, then seeing animals as particular kinds of affections leads to a sympathetic understanding of the possibilities in existence, all existences.

In a way, Swedenborg's way of looking through the material world to the worlds beyond seems almost selfishly man-centered, as though we are the biggest, best, and only thing around. In effect, if we ranked the orders of existence in Swedenborg's terms, the world (including our own body) is one order, our inner experience is the next greatest world, the spiritual worlds beyond this one the next greatest, and God's nature supreme. *Our existence, our experience, is the door to all else.* That is simply the way it is. This doesn't give us cosmic status so much as it gives us cosmic responsibility. But in the hierarchical order of things our existence here is near the bottom. How we are the door to all else (made in the image of God) has been miserably, poorly understood. In a real sense, Swedenborg threw too much light on this. The light was dazzling, blinding, and not well understood. Our experience is the bridge between the material world, in which our body really lives, and the worlds between this and the Divine. Swedenborg was man-centered, but this partly meant responsibility to ourselves and creation, responsibility insofar as we understand it.

This awakening feeling of responsibility for creation is reflected in the concern with conservation of animal species. Progress was about to drain and cement over a pond that housed a rare species of salamander that existed nowhere else on earth. Concerned people saved this pond. The demise of this salamander could have cut the possibilities in creation by one. We are awakening from the feeling that we can take and use whatever part of existence we want, to a more responsible position as custodian.

The Grand Man

Swedenborg revealed that all the multitudes of heaven are organized into societies that are parts of the Grand Man. The whole of heaven is in the form of a man (AC 3624 f.). At first this sounds like a strange and overly anthropomorphic, or man-centered, idea. It has to be examined a little to see how beautiful a conception it is. *We are images of the Grand Man;*

the Grand Man is not an image of us. The Grand Man is all aspects of the humanness of God combined. The hierarchical order is then God, the Divine Human appearing as the Grand Man, our inner humanness, our bodily form. Each person is an edition or image of the Grand Man. Occasionally Swedenborg would get very mystical and say something like "The Lord is Very Man" (DP 65). There are many meanings here. Whatever man is, at the core is God. Or, the other way around, God is man like us, but Very Man—that is, even more essentially what we tend to be.

It is now allowed to relate and describe wonderful things, which, so far as I know, have never as yet been known to anyone, nor even entered into his mind, namely, that the universal heaven is so formed that it corresponds to the Lord, as to His Divine Human; and that man is so formed that, as to all things in general and in particular in him, he corresponds to heaven, and by means of heaven to the Lord. This is a great mystery, which is now to be revealed. AC 3624

Heaven corresponds to the Divine Human. Man, in his mind and body, corresponds in the tiniest particulars to this form. We are an image of the Grand Man. The details of the societies that relate to the eyes, hands, feet, etc., of the Grand Man are the full inner implications of these parts of ourselves. Apparently this is common knowledge in heaven.

It is from this ground that it has been occasionally stated in the preceding pages, where speaking of heaven and angelic societies, that they belonged to some province of the body, as to that of the head, or of the breast, or of the abdomen, or of some particular member or organ; and this by reason of the said correspondence.

That such a correspondence exists, is perfectly well known in in the other life, not only to the angels, but also to spirits, and even to the wicked. The angels are hence acquainted with the most secret things which are in man . . . this I have been enabled to know from this circumstance, that when I spoke of any part of man, they not only know all the structure of that part, its manner of acting and use, but also more innumerable things than man is capable of exploring, yea, of understanding. AC 3625–3626

[T]he whole man in general, and in particular whatever is in man, has such a correspondence, inasmuch that there is not the smallest part, nor even the smallest constituent of a part, which does not correspond . . . and further, that unless there was such a correspondence of man with heaven, and by means of heaven with the Lord, thus with what is prior to himself, and by means of what is prior with the First, he would not subsist a single moment, but would fall into annihilation. AC 3628

Our existence both in general and in particular is a correspondent with heaven, and through the Grand Man of heaven, to the Lord. The Grand Man is the Lord's humanness. And it is made up of the countless multitudes of heaven organized into their innumerable societies of like people. Each society is also in the form of a man because man's form represents a basic combination of functions. The idea staggers the imagination. It turns around all priorities. We are because It is. We are a corresponding image to It. It is the model of our existence, the ultimate of all our possibilities.

In hell there is no Grand Man. The individuals there are cut off from each other and their potentials. They cannot unify into societies "where the joy of one is the joy of all." Hell is dark and fragmented. Heaven is the One.

The kernel of the whole idea of correspondences is that Something is manifesting and showing itself in many ways. This is true whether we speak of the Lord, the Grand Man as the basis of all humanity, or the way in which individuals endlessly cast forth images of themselves.

Swedenborg brought it all together in a few lines. Here he was speaking of all levels of existence simultaneously. At its lowest level he was referring to the experience we each have of ourselves as the center of things.

And furthermore, the universal heaven is such, that every one is as it were the centre of all, for he is the centre of influxes through the heavenly form from all, and hence an image of heaven results to every one, and makes him like to itself, that is, a man; for such as the general is, such is a part of the general; since the parts must needs be like their general, in order to belong thereto. AC 3633

A man who is in correspondence, that is, who is in love to the Lord, and in charity towards the neighbor, and thence in faith, as to his spirit is in heaven, and as to his body, in the world. And as he thus acts in unity with the angels, he is also an image of heaven . . . therefore he is also a little heaven, under a human form. AC 3634

The visible universal is nothing else than a theatre representative of the Lord's kingdom, and that this latter is a theatre representative of the Lord Himself. AC 3483

9

Inner Meanings

It is as though Emanuel Swedenborg had climbed a long way up from the valley floor of our ordinary experience and understanding. He began with rocks and minerals and climbed through all the sciences to the heights of the inner life and from there wandered through all the spiritual worlds. His psychological understanding of the spontaneous inner language of dreams and the hypnogogic state was already notable. Yet his work on the inner meanings contained in the Bible left almost everyone behind as he climbed through the clouds to the top of the mountain. This was his greatest, richest, and most difficult work to follow. I cannot summarize what he found here because it is too extensive. Instead, I would simply like to provide a general understanding of what was involved.

It is clear that this Swedish master felt that his unfolding of the spiritual and celestial meanings hidden in the language of the Bible was his greatest work. But as the theologian Horton points out, great men are not always remembered for what they considered great.[32] Sir Isaac Newton spent much time in alchemy, which is now forgotten alongside his work on celestial mechanics. In this case, however, those who know Swedenborg best would be inclined to agree that his work on the inner meanings of the Bible is his richest and most significant work.

Swedenborg came to theology by an unusual avenue, and this made all the difference. He took up theology while grappling with the spontaneous inner language of correspondences in dreams, in the hypnogogic state, and in trances. How many theologians enter theology in this manner? Hindu and Buddhist theologians may often enter this way, but not western religious figures. Swedenborg's unusual understanding set him apart. To appreciate the greatness of his biblical work, one needs some appreciation and acceptance of the spontaneous inner language of symbolism. Knowledge of the language of the unconscious and an interest in biblical meaning seldom exist in one person; those interested in depth psychology are usually not interested in the Bible and biblical scholars find the language of the unconscious merely a curiosity.

Swedenborg's former real ignorance of biblical meaning was striking in comparison to what he later found. In 1745, Swedenborg was working on *The Word Explained,* an eight-volume work that he wisely chose not to publish. There he tried to penetrate the meaning of the Bible with his own intellect. The work is a relatively dull rehash of conventional ideas. But here and there it has curious references to dreams, spirits, and correspondences. After his enlightenment by the Lord, his first publication was the *Arcana Coelestia (Heavenly Secrets).* The *Arcana* is so rich, deep, and powerful that it hardly looks like the work of the same man who had written *The Word Explained.* Something had happened. His whole understanding had richly flowered in several different directions simultaneously.

Swedenborg could not have been terribly concerned about his public relations image or the *Arcana* would not have been the first published work of this newly enlightened man. The English edition of the first tome of his new understanding runs to twelve volumes and 5,800 pages. These heavenly secrets are staggeringly rich. Even Swedenborg experts often put off reading it and treat it as a literary Mount Everest. On the surface it is mainly an exposition of the inner meanings in Genesis and Exodus. But he also developed parallel meanings from almost every other part of the Bible, so he is coincidentally unlocking the whole of Scripture. It also goes into the dynamics of the inner life of individuals, churches, and Jesus Christ—simultaneously, since these are ultimately one. In addition he intersperses cogent summaries of his findings in heaven and hell. Every other major idea he was to deal with for the next thirty years is contained in the *Arcana.* Swedenborg published it anonymously, as Servant of the Lord Jesus Christ. He sent copies to the learned bishops of the western world. No wonder they didn't take notice! It was simply too rich and too different to be readily understood. Interestingly enough, it was ordinary people who were first impressed by the *Arcana.* This is understandable, for it relates to the kind of meaning Swedenborg was dealing with.

In Swedenborg's time the Holy Bible was the Word of God. Other bibles, such as the Koran, Bhagavad Gita, Tao Te Ching, Dhammapada, were little known and unavailable. Of all the world's bibles, the western Holy Bible is probably by far the most obscure and varied work. There are many indications that it is at least partly a symbolic work. The Lord spoke in a symbolic language of parables, and, indeed, it was predicted the messiah would do this. The massive symbolism of the Book of Revelation had puzzled generations. There is clear symbolism everywhere in it. Isaiah refers to a man as a clay pot that complains of having handles (Isaiah 45:9–13). But how much is symbolic, and of what? Some early biblical scholars treated much of it as an allegory. Allegorical interpretation allowed anyone to find whatever meaning pleased them. Because of these excesses, these allegorical interpretations fell into disfavor. The opposite pole also emerged. The fundamentalists stuck by the literal word as fact. The world was "literally" created in six days.

Swedenborg's approach to the Bible left room for these differences while transcending them. He was very sure that there was a full and useful meaning in the literal words as read by the fundamentalists. In fact, this was the real basis of all the meanings. He said the internal meaning without the external would be like a house without a foundation (HD 262). For those who could not see any further beyond the literal, this meaning was meant to be a sufficient guide.

The key to the deeper meaning lay not so much in the psychological language of correspondences; this only gave one confidence in symbolic language. The key lay in the spirit with which the person came to the Bible. Those who wanted just laws to guide their lives would find laws. Those who wanted to feel the presence of the Lord would find this presence. Those who struggled with understanding the complexities of human experience would find this echoed. Many ordinary people always read the Bible this way. When in trouble and searching for guidance they look in the Bible, confident that it will speak to them as a personal friend and guide. And it does. On the other hand, scholars who are stuffed with facts that a particular book was proven by computer analysis to be made of two separate documents would often find their personal experience of the Bible to founder in this scholarship. Swedenborg approached the Bible through that psychological experience by which it became alive to ordinary persons. Hence, where learned bishops couldn't see any gift in his work, ordinary people could. But whereas ordinary people were sometimes projecting into it and finding meanings appropriate to them, Swedenborg was finding two universal levels of meanings locked within the odd language of the Bible. This does not contravene what ordinary people feel in the Bible, for I believe what they feel and what he is talking about are aspects of the same process. But where they are searching, Swedenborg was moving with great certainty and scholarship, under the guidance of heaven.

Swedenborg said that only the Lord inwardly instructs on the meaning of the Word. He clearly said that he was not instructed by any spirit or angel on what the Word meant; he was only instructed by the Lord. But this is true of everyone. The secret of unlocking the Bible lays in the spirit with which it is approached. Those who love truth for its own sake (not to show off their knowledge) and apply it in their lives will be shown. Being ready to apply it and use it was for Swedenborg a critical sign that the individual really wanted to know. Belief became real as act, not just an airy intellectual process.

Swedenborg used the term "Word" in more senses than just the printed Bible. He also used it in the deeper Hebrew sense of what causes all things to be (WH 17). This is the Word that existed before anything was (John 1:1). One might say that the Word is the power of the Lord to form and guide. Those who approach the Bible with this deeper longing or searching will meet in it the power of God to guide them. Knock and it will be opened. The proof of understanding is in what the person does. What is real must exist. The Word of God becomes act or uses. So Swedenborg was really dealing with this heartbeat of understanding. As a result, those who engaged in a heartfelt search in the Bible were instructed by the Lord Himself, who was their life. Whether this understanding was cloudy and fumbling in personal meaning or striking the real gold of the Lord's inner meaning, they were moving in the same direction. These heartfelt personal fumblings could feel the power of the inner levels of meaning Swedenborg was referring to.

Swedenborg read the Bible in its original languages. The

indexes of the day didn't satisfy him, so he made his own. He spent years on it. In fact, through most of his late years, the Bible was reported to be the only book visible in his study. He combined tremendous singleminded scholarship with experience of the Lord in heaven to produce one of the most profound understandings of the Bible ever offered. Indeed, its very richness, breadth, and depth is an impediment to anything but a wholehearted attempt to follow his lead. Many who gave his work a cursory glance dismissed it as allegorical (which it is not) or as denying the sense of the letter (which he held sacred).

Swedenborg found that most of the Bible contained, within the outer sense of the letter, two further levels of meaning. The significant books in the Old Testament are the five books of Moses, Joshua, Judges, the two books of Samuel, the two Kings, the Psalms of David and the prophets Isaiah, Jeremiah, the Lamentations, Ezekiel, Daniel, Hosea, Joel, Amos, Obadiah, Jonah, Micah, Nahum, Habakkuk, Zephaniah, Haggai, Zechariah and Malachi. In the New Testament books with such an inner meaning are Matthew, Mark, Luke, John and Revelation (HD 266). Job has an inner meaning but it is disconnected. This list includes most of the Old Testament and all but the works of Paul in the New Testament.

In effect, the Bible is the revealed Word, structured so as to be understood simultaneously by man and angels in the spiritual and celestial heavens. When man reads it in its literal sense, spiritual and celestial angels simultaneously understand it in the higher meanings appropriate to their realms. The Bible is the revealed Word through all the worlds. Swedenborg mostly elaborates upon the spiritual sense because men can partly see and understand it. But the celestial sense "can be explained only with difficulty, for it does not fall so much into the thought of the understanding as into the affection of the will" (DS 19). In other words, the celestial sense is in feeling and doing. It rises above words.

From the Lord proceeds the celestial heaven, and out of that the spiritual and out of that the natural world. These are all levels of meaning contained in the Bible.

This is the nature of the Word. In its ultimate sense it is natural, in its interior sense it is spiritual, and in its inmost sense it is celestial; and in each it is Divine. That the Word is of this nature is not apparent in the sense of the Letter, as this is natural; because man when in the world has hitherto not known anything concerning the heavens; and consequently has not known what the spiritual is, and what the celestial. DS 6

The difference between these degrees cannot be known unless by a knowledge of correspondence. For these three degrees are quite distinct from each other, like end, cause and effect. DS 7

This inner meaning is the same as the mystical meaning. Swedenborg senses the difficulty in getting it across to people.

The Jews and also some Christians believe, indeed, that in these, and also in the rest of the passages of the Word, there is some meaning stored up, which they call mystical, the reason of this belief being an idea of holiness in regard to the Word has been impressed upon them from early childhood; but when they are asked what this mystical meaning is, they do not know. If they are told that because the Word is Divine, this meaning must necessarily be such as is in the heaven among the angels: and that no other mystical meaning can exist in the Word . . . and, furthermore, that this mystical meaning which is in heaven among the angels is nothing else than what is called spiritual and celestial, and treats solely of the Lord, of His kingdom, and of the church, consequently, of good and truth; and that if they knew what good and truth, or what faith and love, are, they would be able to know this meaning—when they are told this scarcely anyone believes it. In fact, so ignorant, at the present day, are those who belong to the church, that what is related concerning the celestial and spiritual is scarcely comprehensible to them. Be it so; nevertheless as it has been granted me, of the Lord's Divine mercy, to be at the same time in heaven as a spirit and on earth as a man, and therefore to speak with angels, and this now continually for many years, I cannot but open up those things of the Word that are called mystical, that is, its interior things, which are the spiritual and celestial things of the Lord's kingdom. AC 4923

It took a man who had direct and long association with angels to come to see and learn the wide acceptance in heaven of this inner meaning. Because the Word is written in correspondences, it permits a conjunction of man with the heavens and with the Lord through the Word.

The preceding chapter dealt with the breadth of the idea of correspondences, or symbolic language. It is an ancient and very common idea, having appeared at various times as the source of pictographic writing, myth, occult sciences, ceremony, and even modern plays and poetry, psychosomatic medicine, and projective tests.

What seems mysterious is that the symbol reaches beyond the simple things. It represents a host of circumstances that may occur anywhere, anytime. The symbolic ceremonial occasion represents all occasions. The dynamism of the symbol lives insofar as it echoes in a person. Witness ancient symbols whose sense we have now lost. They became just museum artifacts of a past age. An example would be a Cretan figure of the Magna Mater. The little clay figure represented all the possibilities of motherliness. Volumes could be written of its implications. The symbol only lives within the one who feels its implications. True idolatry was rarely practiced. Just as the Roman Catholic genuflects before a plaster Virgin Mary, because of *what* is being represented, primitives also genuflected before their symbols, keys to larger worlds. Thus, in a complex, this is what Swedenborg's language of biblical correspondences is involved with. It relates to the most ancient, honorable, and varied traditions. The daring aspect is that he was unlocking the western world's key of keys.

In the first paragraph of *Heaven and Hell,* Swedenborg unfolded the spiritual meaning of a familiar biblical passage.

Immediately after the tribulation of those days shall the sun be darkened, and the moon shall not give her light, and the stars shall fall from heaven, and the powers of the heavens shall be shaken; and then shall appear the sign of the Son of man in heaven; and then shall all the tribes of the earth mourn; and they shall see the Son of man coming in the clouds of heaven with great power and great glory. And he shall send his angels and a trumpet and a great voice, and they shall gather together his elect from the four winds, from one end of the heavens to the other. Matthew 24:29–31

Those who understand the sense of the letter understand that someday, in a cosmic falling apart of things, Jesus will come and gather his elect together. It is a someday, cataclysmic, final judgment. This is the literal sense of the letter. It is true and sacred. Yet there is an inner spiritual sense. Swedenborg described it as it applies to churches. I would like to translate it downward to the individual. This is possible because the spiritual sense applies equally to the Lord, the heavens, churches, and individuals; "for the Word of The Lord is such that wherever it treats of one person, it treats of all men, and of each individual, with a difference according to the disposition of each: this being the universal sense of the Word" (AC 838). Man is a church in the least form. Churches are the ultimates of heaven and represent heaven. Heaven is a representative of the Lord. The spiritual sense carries within it all these levels of meaning. The celestial sense is more difficult to describe, since it is more like feeling and doing than it is ideas. In terms of a person-church the passage reads as follows:

BIBLE	SPIRITUAL SENSE
Immediately after the tribulation of those days	When the man-church has come to its end, its extreme state

shall the sun be darkened,	God-love-feeling will no longer be known.
the moon shall not give her light,	Faith, or all our ideas of how things are, will fall into darkness
and the stars shall fall from heaven,	all the little guides we had will fail us
And the powers of the heavens shall be shaken;	it is a total, awesome and terrible change
and then shall appear the sign of the Son of man in heaven;	In this extreme state each shall know the root of humanness.
and then shall all the tribes of the earth mourn;	The man will be in total mourning
and they shall see the Son of man coming in the clouds of heaven with great power and great glory.	reduced to his most extreme state, in the clouds of his understanding, shall appear the Only Man, the only power left.
And he shall send his angels with a trumpet and a great voice,	Out of this Only One, will come powers to rescue the man—
and they shall gather together his elect from the four winds, from one end of the heavens to the other. (Matthew 24:29–31)	what remains of good in the man (the elect) will be united into a One.

A few comments will deepen an appreciation of the correspondences involved. "Those days" here refers to any day of great tribulation. The passage is speaking spiritually of any man, any church, any time. The spiritual meaning transcends time and is speaking of a general truth. "The sun" that is darkened refers to the Lord. The main light will no longer shine. Angels know the Lord as the sun of heaven. "The moon" shines by light reflected from the sun. This is like faith, whose source of light is the Lord-Sun. Or this relates to thought or faith (reflected, light of moon) being secondary to feeling (sun), to the One Life. God is primal, we are secondary. Love-feeling is primal; without it the light-heat goes out of faith, all the dim light we have of ideas that guide us. The meaning is similar to the stars' fall. There is nothing left to guide the person-church. He is reduced to a most extreme state. The Son of man is a primitive idea whose meaning we've almost lost. Most everyone takes it to mean Jesus Christ, which is one level of meaning. God is the Only Man. The Son of man is the representative of this one. It might be called the core of the individual personal identity. Swedenborg says that the phrase "Son of man" is consistently used where redemption, salvation, reformation, and regeneration are spoken of (DL 23). This is the core of meaning of this passage. The church's-man's salvation is being spoken of. "Clouds of heaven" easily represents our foggy, clouded understanding of what is really happening in this extreme state. "Trumpet and a great voice" easily represents the overwhelming powers the man-church is caught in. "Four winds" is an ancient idea: four represents all places—the total—and is related to the four points of the compass. Jung and many oriental religions represent the fundamental Self as a fourfold mandala.

This passage, then, is speaking symbolically or representatively of everyone's situation when they've really had it. It is the picture of the extreme limit of personal loss, and something coming from beyond the self to rescue the person. It happens to everyone. It happens to churches when they go through the agony of dying. It is an everyone, all places, all times description of what happens in the extremes of dying and coming to life again. Bear in mind that Swedenborg is not undoing or violating the literal meaning. That stands as true. But whereas the sense of the letter seems to be speaking of a once-someday cataclysmic event, in a spiritual sense it is describing what almost everyone has known and will know. The awesome sweep and power of Swedenborg's insights into the spiritual meaning come from this. *It is alive and true for everyone. It will always be true. It is the nature of things.* Hence it is sacred, or terribly valuable. It is perfectly appropriate for each to think back on the most extreme situation in his life and see the parallels with this passage. Then it no longer seems simply like picturesque speech but more like an awesome picture of reality.

Another example illustrates what Swedenborg found. The scene is from Genesis. The prophet Noah, warned of a flood, has built an ark that contains all life in it. The image of a man gathering up all his life and trying to weather a great storm should not be too difficult to recognize. The person is trying to weather great difficulty. "Noah" literally means "rest." It is unfortunate that these meanings, which are apparent to those who read Hebrew, are lost in the translation.[33] Noah is appropriate in several senses. He is, in effect, the remaining one, the rest, the one left over, what survives. In the story he is also concerned to find a place to rest. In its inner meaning this relates to the man in adversity trying to find what is right and good, where he may rest. Noah has suffered through a long period of storm. His vessel comes to rest on Mount Ararat (light). His troubles aren't over, for other than the light that holds up his vessel (his life) there is no place to rest. The rest of the earth is flooded. The psychological issue is how the man who has locked up himself against adversity can finally find rest and freedom.

BIBLE	SPIRITUAL SENSE
And it came to pass at the end of forty days	At the end of a complete period of trial
that Noah opened the window of the ark which he had made	he made an effort to understand his situation (open the window)
and he sent forth a raven,	he acted out of doubt and falsity (raven, black, ignorance, falsity).

and it went forth going and returning	he was uncertain and ambivalent.
until the waters were dried up from off the earth	His situation remained as before till the Lord made it better.
and he sent forth a dove from him	And he expressed a gentle hope
to see if the waters were abated from off the faces of the ground.	to see if he would be permitted to begin life again.
And the dove found no rest for the sole of her foot.	His hope found no place to be.
And she returned unto him to the ark, for the waters were on the faces of the whole earth;	so he withdraws into himself again. Adversity still reigns.
and he put forth his hand and took her, and brought her unto him in the ark.	He still acts by his own powers to protect himself.
And he stayed yet other seven days; and again he sent forth the dove out of the ark;	He awaits God's time and will, and tries again
And the dove came back to him at eventide	And hope shows just the beginning
and lo, in her mouth an olive leaf plucked off	She shows (mouth) a little (leaf) of love's (olive) faith (plucked off).
So Noah knew that the waters were abated from off the earth.	The ground of being is less covered now by falsity and doubt.
And he stayed yet other seven days and sent forth the dove and she returned not again unto him anymore. Genesis 8:6–13	He awaits God's will and this time finds freedom.

He is shortly to find rest on the ground that permits his life (the animals in the ark) to be free. Resting on a mountain of light, or on the beginning of understanding, in the midst of adversity he first sends out a black bird, the raven. The raven has often been seen as symbolic of death or at least great difficulty. After so much adversity, what he sends out is black. This black mood (doubt, ignorance) didn't find ground. Then he sends out a dove, which is more representative of gentle hope or even of the Holy Spirit. The bird goes out and back (hope, ambivalence, withdrawal again into the ark). Just to show Swedenborg's scholarship, he examined in detail just the matter of Noah taking the dove in hand and returning it to the ark. For pages he shows dozens of biblical quotes using the word "hand," which, as we saw earlier, means personal power: "Noah shall spread forth his hands in the midst of them, as he that swimmeth spreadeth forth his hand to swim, and he shall lay low his pride together with the devices of his hands (Isaiah 25:11). Here hands denotes man's own power, from regarding himself as above others, thus from his pride" AC 878. Swedenborg goes into seventeen other biblical passages showing the use of hands to denote personal power. The reader begins to get a sense of the consistency of biblical symbolism. The hand representing personal power doesn't seem so strange; so in putting forth his hand and taking the dove, he was still acting by his personal powers. The man of the church doesn't find ground until he acts from what transcends him. Under this analysis the tiniest details come to life. Why a raven at first and a dove later? Now we know. The faces of the ground is an unusual experience. Swedenborg says face corresponds to mind (AC 4791, 4805); face (surface, what appears) equals mind; faces of the ground, the superficial appearance of what supports our existence. Noah, the survivor of great trials and temptations, is still thinking superficially. But he is looking for the faces of the ground, where his life can begin again. It would be nice to release the pent-up life in the ark and find some ground to rely upon instead of being perched so long in stress and uncertainty. Again, this is an image of every man. Everyone has been locked up in his own life concerns, trying to survive adversity. Each seeks some outside ground, somewhere to rest. Noah waited another seven days (a whole, complete period, i.e., until God wills) and this time the dove came back with a freshly plucked olive leaf. The olive was symbolic of love to the ancients because of the pleasant sensual quality of its oil. Rest is given in God's time (40 days, plus 7, plus 7). This only touches upon the meanings in this passage. There is much more. Christ was tempted for forty days. The earth was made in seven. But the basic meaning can be seen of man in adversity, waiting, sending out hope after hope, only finding rest in God's time. The whole passage refers to the regeneration or remaking of man in the spiritual sense. Everyone has been locked up in his own life and concerns and seeks some outside ground, somewhere to rest.

I hope the reader is getting a sense of how often this spiritual language is speaking of man's intimate experiences. These excerpts leave out Swedenborg's tremendous scholarship and gradual unfolding of ideas that make the spiritual interpretation more convincing. Swedenborg isn't drawing on chance connections. If you doubt that taking the dove into his hand and putting it in the ark means withdrawing into his own powers, then he amply reviews the use of "hand" in the Bible to show its inner meaning. But most of all, these quaint ancient stories come alive in the tiniest details of everyone's life. If Swedenborg is correct, it is appalling that so much meaning should be locked up and forgotten in an ancient book.

Let us examine the inner implications of the well-known opening passage of Genesis. On the surface it describes the six days of creation of the earth, all life and man. In its symbolic sense it is speaking of the inner nature of man, churches, and the essential livingness of existence. The earth created is man, any person. It is speaking of the always true, the nature of things, what can be confirmed by any life. I realize that without some experience with the symbolic language of the unconscious, the interpretation given here will seem to some to be reaching too far, to be a bit farfetched. Another disadvantage is that the few passages interpreted here Swedenborg backs up with thirty-two pages of careful development of meaning and numerous biblical parallels. Yet even those inexperienced in this kind of language may at least see the possibility that Swedenborg may have found two new levels of meaning. Again, these new levels do not contradict or contravene the literal meanings. The literal is true, but the spiritual is also true, a matter of truths within truths. Swedenborg makes clear that there are also celestial levels of meaning, the common understanding of celestial angels. These are like myriads to one, and beyond a simple exposition. In these interpretations I have taken the liberty to follow Swedenborg's meanings and also to clarify them in the direction of psychological meaning in modern terms.

BIBLE	SPIRITUAL SENSE
In the beginning God created the heavens and the earth.	Life begins when God creates the internal man (heaven, the higher aspect) and the external man (earth, body, lower aspect).
And the earth was a void and emptiness, and thick darkness was upon the faces of the deep.	The external man begins in great ignorance and instinctuality (darkness upon the faces of the deep).

Just as an example of a similar linking of man's ignorance and void-emptiness, Swedenborg quotes Jeremiah: "My people is stupid, they have not known me; they are foolish sons, are not intelligent; they are wise to do evil, but to do good they have no knowledge. I beheld the earth, and lo a void and emptiness" (Jeremiah 4:22–23).

And the spirit of God moved upon the faces of the waters.	And the life of God animates man's unconscious tendencies

(waters equal all the potential within mind, faces of waters equal tendencies, waves, currents).

And God said, let there be light, and there was light.	And God created awareness (God said—God's will takes the form of let there be—and there was. We are seeing an active creation of the Lord).
And God saw the light, that it was good,	And the Divine is aware of the goodness (or use) of this creation,
and God distinguished between the light and the darkness. And God called the light day, and the darkness He called night.	which begins to make fundamental distinctions between what is full awareness and of God (daylight) and limited awareness and of man (night).
And the evening and the morning were the first day.	From the darkness to the morning of awareness is called the first day of creation.

It begins to be apparent that some kind of unfolding has started that begins by the distinction of some great polar opposites, heaven-earth, day-night, light-darkness. The distinction is between a higher and lower, or a fullness of understanding as against a limitation.

And God said, let there be an expanse in the midst of the waters, and let it distinguish between the waters and the waters.	The internal of man is opened up (expanse in the midst of the waters) and from it the distinction of the internal and the external man (between waters and waters).

Later we will see that one of the waters gives birth to land, which is the firmer, ego consciousness.

And the evening and the morning were the second day.

And this growth of awareness is the second day of creation.

And God said, let the waters under the heaven be gathered together to one place, and let the dry land appear; and it was so.

This distinguishes what is of God (waters under heaven) and man's consciousness (dry land appears).

And God called the dry land earth, and the gathering together of the waters called He seas; the God saw that it was good.

And man's consciousness is his place (earth) and the rest is his potential (seas). This process is good. (It is good that man has a place in the midst of the seas to work from.)

And God said, let the earth

Out of God's will, as tho from the man himself

bring forth the tender herb,

appears the beginnings of ideas (outgrowths of consciousness)

the herb yielding seed and the fruit-tree bearing fruit after its kind whose seed is in itself, upon the earth.

which have more and more life in themselves in man's consciousness (upon the earth).

And it was so.

This follows God's will.

And the earth brought forth the tender herb, the herb yielding seed after its kind, and the tree bearing fruit, whose seed is in itself, after its kind;

(It reemphasizes that this growth appears to arise from man himself even though it follows God's will.)

and God saw it was good.

The Divine sees the good in this process.

And the evening and morning were the third day.

This is the third day or stage in the creation of man.

At this point the higher and lower aspects of man are distinguished and his thinking begins to bear fruit as though through his own powers.

And God said, let there be lights in the expanse of the heavens,	God willed that there be awarenesses (light) in the internal man (expanse of heaven).
to distinguish between the day and the night;	Which makes basic distinctions,
and let them be for signs and for seasons, and for days, and for years;	which will always serve as a guide
and let them be for lights in the expanse of the heavens,	in the internal of understanding
to give light upon the earth;	to guide the limited ego consciousness,
and it was so.	and God's will is realized.
And God made two great lights,	And God made two great guides,
the great light to rule by day,	love/will (sun, warmth, heat) to guide in the most direct way (by day)
and the lesser light to rule by night;	and faith/understanding (moon, reflected light of sun) to guide in less clear circumstances
and the stars.	and the myriad of tiny guides in the less clear circumstances.
And God set them in the expanse of the heavens,	And God made these an integral part of the inner man
to give light upon the earth.	to guide the limited consciousness ego.

And to rule in the day, and in the night, and to distinguish between the light and the darkness	To rule the full understanding (day) or the limited (night) and to distinguish truth (light) and falsity (darkness).
and God saw it was good.	And the Divine sees the good in this (through all lives, in all creation).
And the evening and the morning were the fourth day.	And this is the fourth stage or day of man's development.

At this point man functions with useful ideas of his own (tender herbs) and has the massive internal guidance system of love-will–Divine good, and when this isn't functioning (at night), the lesser guides of faith-understanding-intellect.

And God said, let the waters cause to creep forth the creeping things, the living soul;	Now the man begins to live. (Prior to this his life was inanimate, i.e., dry land, plants. Now he begins to live, i.e., acts within the love/will of God.)
and let fowl fly above the earth	And begins to have perspective on the lesser aspects of his life
upon the faces of the expanse of the heavens.	which is the surface of the inner man.
And God created great whales.	Out of the unconscious (the sea) is created great forces with much life in them (great whales).
And every living soul that creepeth,	And every living tendency
which the waters made to creep forth,	that comes out of the unconscious
after their kinds, and every winged fowl after its kind;	is interrelated after its kinds

and God saw it was good.	and the Divine sees the use in this.
And God blessed them, saying, be fruitful and multiply,	This life from God seems to have love (fruitful) and understanding (multiply) in itself
and fill the waters in the seas, and the fowl shall be multiplied in the earth.	and fills the mind (waters in the seas) and experience of man (the earth).
And the evening and the morning were the fifth day.	And this is the fifth stage in the creation of man.
And God said, let the earth bring forth the living soul after its kind,	There emerged from man (earth) living tendencies,
the beast, and the moving thing	instincts and feelings,
and the wild animal of the earth after its kind; and it was so.	and pleasures of the senses.
And God made the wild animal after its kind, and the beast after its kind, and everything that creepeth on the ground after its kind;	And these became real and seem to arise from their own kind, gentle affections from the gentle, and sense pleasure from the sensual,
and God saw it was good.	and the Divine saw the use in this.
And God said, let us make man in our image, after our likeness;	This man is to be like God.

In the most ancient church, with the members of which the Lord conversed face to face, the Lord appeared as a man; concerning which much might be related, but the time has not yet arrived. On this account they called no one "man" but the Lord Himself, and the things which pertained to Him; neither did they call themselves "men. . . ." Hence in the Prophets, by "man" and the "Son of man," in the highest sense, is meant the Lord; and, in the internal sense, wisdom and intelligence. AC 49 and let them have dominion over the fish of the sea, and over the fowl of the heavens, and over the beast, and over all the earth, and over every creeping thing that creepeth upon the earth.

and have dominion over all aspects of his life.

And God created man in his own image

and is given the power of understanding

in the image of God created He him;

and will.

male and female created He them.

Understanding and will, the two that can be one.

What was meant by "male and female," in the internal sense, was well known to the most Ancient Church, but when the interior sense of the Word was lost among their posterity, this arcanum also perished. Their marriages were their chief sources of happiness and delight, and whatever admitted of the comparison they likened to marriage. . . . The understanding in the spiritual man they therefore called male and the will female, and when these acted as one they called it a marriage. AC 54

And God blessed them, and God said unto them, Be fruitful, and multiply,

Such a man is to do what is good (fruitful) and true (multiply),

and replenish the earth

which is to benefit to the whole person,

and subdue it;

by bringing him into control

and have dominion over the fish of the sea, and over the fowl of the heavens, and over every living thing that creepth upon the earth.

and dominion over all his tendencies.

And God said, Behold I give you every herb bearing seed which is upon the faces of all the earth, and every tree in which is fruit; the tree yielding seed, to you it shall be for food.

He is given every truth which regards use (herb bearing seed), the good of faith (tree which is in fruit) and spiritual guidance (tree yielding seed).

And to every wild animal of the earth, and to every fowl of the heavens, and to everything that creepeth upon the earth, wherein there is a living soul, I give every green herb for food; and it was so.

To every aspect of the man in which there is spiritual life (a living soul) the Lord gives spiritual food (green herb).

And God saw everything that He had made, and behold it was very good.

God saw all the implications in what He had done, and it was very good.

And the evening and the morning were the sixth day.

And this is the progression to the sixth day of creation.

There are many other meanings in this section of Genesis, some of which Swedenborg touched on, some of which he only implied. Basically the section is dealing, in the internal sense, with the development of a person from complete spiritual ignorance (void and empty) to the beginning differentiation of what is from God (the heavens) and man (earth), to greater and greater understanding, livingness (plants, fish, animals), to the man who becomes the image of God. This man still has much to do to subdue and come into control over his tendencies. These six days of creation have not yet reached the seventh day in which the man can rest.

It would be sufficient, for my purposes, if the reader sees only the possibility that familiar passages may have another inner, more psychological and spiritual level of meaning. To really appreciate this level requires some spiritual search, a need to know. Missing here is Swedenborg's comparison with parallel passages and his careful scholarship. He also referred to ancient practices that throw light on the inner meaning. Without this, for instance, it isn't immediately apparent how male and female are related to understanding and will, nor the happy marriage of these, in which what one understands and believes is made real by will or action, hence bringing fruitfulness and multiplication into one's life. Faith is made real by charity, and this is called a happy marriage. Whereas we have to struggle somewhat to grasp this spiritual language, angels find it easier, as illustrated by an incident in heaven Swedenborg reported.

Certain ones were taken up to the first entrance-court of heaven, when I was reading the Word, and from there conversed with me. They said they could not there understand one whit of any word or letter therein, but only what was signified in the nearest interior sense, which they declared to be so beautiful, in such order of sequence, and so affecting them, that they called it Glory. AC 65

Swedenborg's exegetical works are too rich and varied to be simply summarized. Since spirit and life are much the same, the inner sense is always closer to the nooks and crannies of human experience and human travail. This inner sense is speaking of life, everyone's life, of churches, of Christ's life, of the Lord. In a fundamental way each is the Lord trying to find his way back home.

Swedenborg's thesis of inner meaning is decidedly too rich, too extensive, and too important to be dismissed out of hand. He almost requires the reader to be in a real spiritual search, to learn the symbolic language of the inner life, and then to study the Bible and its inner meanings at great length before a judgment can be made. But this much can be said. Those who have found this inner thread of meaning find that the Bible is incredibly rich, accurate, and relevant to our everyday life.

Though at times Swedenborg's exegesis seems stiff and repetitious, he has his finger on symbolic processes that are still native to man in dreams. Much of this biblical symbolism can still be found in man, though this is not widely known. We have lost touch with these processes, which Swedenborg said the ancients knew quite well, which some primitives understand today, and which are also the natural language of the unconscious.

Swedenborg's biblical exegesis is the richest part of his works, making up a half or better of his theological works. The very richness of this side of his work is another sign that old Emanuel had really journeyed far.

10

The One Present

Essentially Swedenborg was attempting to understand and describe all of life. His personal journey went through the sciences and psychology to the most general understanding possible in the wisdom of theology. By examining separate aspects of Swedenborg's works at a time, I have perhaps presented too static a picture of the whole. Now I want to show something of the whole canvas that Swedenborg has painted.

The first issue is what kind of knowledge is involved in his theological works and on what authority was it presented? Swedenborg remained the same empiricist who had earlier described the mining and smelting of copper and all the other sciences even when he was dealing with the subtleties of the inner world. At no point in his later critical psychological-theological works was he theorizing or speculating. He could illustrate any point by personal experiences, often too numerous to detail. As a psychologist he was closest to the phenomenologist, who is really content to discover and describe the shape of human experience. Although this is Swedenborg's experience, he was potentially describing all of human experience. Nothing need be taken on his authority. Each person can check it for himself because he is referring to the generally real.

If we look at these works as essentially theological the issues remain the same. It is possible, though not common, for everyone to experience the higher worlds and the existence of God. As our understanding of the psychological inner nature of these worlds deepens, the experience comes closer to each of us. In some way Swedenborg saw farther and clearer than most, but what he brought back helped others to see almost as well.

Though Swedenborg had much social intercourse with angels, spirits, and demons, he clearly indicated that he was ultimately only instructed by the Lord. The Lord is the ultimate authority, the Bible is the revealed authority for what he has to say, but ultimately this refers back to the form of human experience. The spiritual world, the Bible, and human experience are interrelated aspects of one reality, life itself. In a real sense Swedenborg is a latter-day prophet and revelator, and like his ancient predecessors, his task is not to break with ancient traditions in a new breed of understanding, but simply to deepen our understanding of ancient traditions. To attack him is not to attack a peculiar breed of thinking, but to attack the real meaning of depth of the ancient tradition. Swedenborg regarded himself as simply a messenger, or a servant, of the Lord. It was clear that he was not to be venerated in any respect for this august role. The celestial angels abhor any attempt to give them credit for their wisdom, and Swedenborg was the same. If there is any good in his work it is God's, not his. His gift from God extends back into the ancient understandings of men (and Swedenborg greatly complemented the primitives) and forward into our understanding based on our own experience. The real basis of authority for his work is, then, in this rich understanding and experience of the Lord, the Bible, ancient traditions, and our present experience. Those who understand Swedenborg partially tend to take apart these realms. Swedenborg dealt with them as essentially one, which for lack of a better term might be called "life."

These two aspects—the personal nature of human experience, which can be checked by everyone, and the nature of the spiritual worlds beyond this one—come together, for one is the inside of the other. *The spiritual worlds beyond this one are the essential nature and potentiality of human experience.* That is simply why Swedenborg could study dreams, the hypnogogic, and trance states and stumble upon spirits interacting with man. That is why psychotics who have partially lost their orientation in relation to this world can find themselves pulled hither and thither by the same spirits who are the unconscious potentials of every person. We are already in the presence of heaven and hell. Heaven and hell in their innermost nature illustrate our present and future potentials. Rightly understood, the whole of our existence is spiritual. We are, or everything is, because God is, which is understanding spiritually. Spiritual understanding is the inner or more general aspect of psychological or personal understanding. Swedenborg has discovered the one real, the unitary, or only system. Though we can separate out different aspects, it is really one life we are dealing with. To those who are accustomed to and comfortable with interacting parts, this very oneness can be a stumbling block. If one must take it apart, levels of correspondence is one way of doing it. We can look at a plant and try to see how it corresponds with and is an ultimate sign of the spiritual world. As we examine its form, color, fruitfulness, etc., we are beginning to sense those aspects of ourselves that empathize with the plant. Through this livingness, which is ourselves, we can begin to sense the nature of the spiritual worlds. Correspondence emphasizes the hierarchical ordering of existence, yet our experience of correspondence drifts toward the unitary expe-

rience of life. The taking apart into aspects is to aid understanding, but the experiential aspect tends to be unitary,
which Swedenborg called life and humanness.

Table 1 shows the hierarchy of existence, with the parallels
between the worlds beyond this one and inner experiences.
The hierarchy of other worlds is also a hierarchy of reality.
The Lord is the Only Real that creates out of Himself the
whole of existence. God's is not a contingent existence like
all other existences. In a sense each higher level is more real
than the level below it. Each level is real in itself, but each
reflects by correspondence higher levels that are progres-
sively more generally true, comprehensive, and free. The
Lord is the free itself, the ultimate truth, the deepest aspect
of humanness. Humanness is the experiential aspect of the

Hierarchy of the Real		As Humanness
The Lord		The innermost nature and highest potential of humanness
The three hells: the opposite possibilities	Celestial heaven	The ultimate of peace, love, and unity with all.
	Spiritual heaven	The ultimate of loving others.
	Spiritual/natural heaven of human potentials	Beginning of realization
World of spirits		Unconscious tendencies, affects, subconscious
Man on earth		Ego awareness
The natural world		Man's acts, the ultimate limitations of human existence

Table 1. The parallels between the hierarchy of real worlds and humanness.

hierarchy of worlds. The material world is not put down in this conception, for it is the ultimate sign and final proof of God's will.

There is a beautiful mystical element running through Swedenborg. By mystical I mean simply what is very great coming into the limited here-now. For me, this mystical element entered when Swedenborg spoke of the humanness of the Lord. He gently put his finger on where in all of varied existence the Lord is to be most intimately known: in the very inner connection of humanness to the Divine. There is the pulse of the relationship.

[U]nless God were a man the universe could not have been created. Bring your thought into the angelic idea of God as being a Man, putting away, as much as you can, the idea of space, and you will come near in thought to the truth. In fact, some of the learned have a perception of spirits and angels as not in space, because they have a perception of the spiritual apart from space. For the spiritual is like thought, which although it is in man, man is nevertheless able by means of it to be present as it were elsewhere, in any place however remote. . . . The Human is the inmost in every created thing. DLW 285

God is very Man, from whom every man is a man according to his reception of love and wisdom. DLW 289

Man, thought, spirit are in the image of God. God is the Very Man. The way to God is through humanness, because it is our closest approach to the Divine. The Lord is the very core of ourselves.

[N]othing lives except God-Man, that is, the Lord. DLW 301

God is a man, and consequently He is God existing; not existing from Himself but in Himself. He who has existence in Himself is God from whom all things are. DLW 16

From this fact that God is a man, all angels and all spirits, in their complete form, are men. This results from the form of heaven, which is like itself in its greatest and in its least parts. DLW 11

I go over and over these little gems, seeing new facets each time. Heaven, man, God-Man are images of Itself in its greatest and least parts. It is like a truth that cannot help but echo itself, however varied its manifestations.

Much religious doctrine puts God beyond any possible grasp. A central meaning of these passages is that God as a man or humanness cannot be missed. Are we not thoroughly human? Though humanness may be like a bottomless well, containing more than can be described, yet it can be known because we are it. I believe this same tendency to know God through humanness is reflected in all the religions in which God comes as a man (Christianity, Hinduism, Buddhism, and others).

In the ultimates of heaven all the things seen and heard are representative of such things as the angels in the higher heavens speak or think. . . . Such things are representative in the ultimates of heaven, because those who are in these ultimates do not comprehend the interior things of angelic wisdom, but they comprehend only such things as represent them. It is also according to Divine Order, that when higher things flow into lower, they are turned into similar things, and in that way presented before the external senses and thus accommodated to the apprehension of everyone. AC 10126

As a person, I am one of these representations. Through my mind I see representations emerging from the inner to show up in images. Or the things of the world are representations of me. I too seem to represent. It is all a representation. How vast!

[A]nd furthermore, the universal heaven is such, that everyone is as it were the centre of all, for he is the centre of influxes through

the heavenly form from all, and hence an image of heaven results
to everyone, and makes him like to itself, that is, a man; for such
as the general is, such is a part of the general. AC 3633

The only One and very Self is omnipresent, omniscient and
omnipotent. This only One and very Self is the Lord-from-eternity
or Jehovah. DP 157

This mystical here-nowness of Swedenborg shows throughout his works. To recognize it one need only sense how
concretely Swedenborg was referring to the reality of the
Divine.

What shall we call the One? Names are culturally bound
to time, place, history. Swedenborg refers to hundreds of
names of the Divine, especially in the manifold language of
correspondences. It is a convention to refer to the Lord as
a male: as He or Father, because our language tends to be
sexually either/or. In Taoism the Him aspect of the Divine
refers to the power to create, make, do. It would be equally
possible to speak of the Her aspect. The Divine Her refers to
the steady, quiet sustainer of creation, much like a mother
that cares for household and children. It would be easy to
argue that the Her God is the more critical, for She gently
sustains creation. Iungerich points out that Swedenborg
found both aspects of the Divine.[34]

I am not particularly wedded to any one name, partly
because of the battles over the names Christ, Allah, Brahma,
Buddha. Surely each of these, referring to the All, must be
the same? In a way I like the ancient Jewish tradition of
having a name for God that was not pronounceable, except
by the rare one who could shout the name as an eruption of
his whole being. Once, in a vision, I heard it pronounced in
a way that could awaken the very rocks. Swedenborg shows
that the ancient use of names really meant nature, or the
essential quality of the person named. A person was called
by whatever fit his nature. In this inner, more living sense of

name-nature, the One could be called by whatever the person experienced as the nature. Or the One might be called the Only, Here-Now, Very Real, and, even as Swedenborg does, Very Human. The name-nature can even be concretely defined simply by the doing of any good act, for good is the name-nature of the One. The higher the good done the better this name-nature is pronounced.

Swedenborg reported that in heaven the Lord appears as a sun. Good angels always have it in their sight, however they turn. This sun is a high image or representation of the Lord, which radiates as its heat and light divine love and wisdom. This divine love is the life of heaven, and through heaven each person's actual life. Our feeling of livingness is, then, this love itself. It is impossible to not know it, since it is ourselves. At most we can limit ourselves by denying it is anything more than just me—as though I make and hold up my own life, and all the good I do is wholly my own creation.

Our own sun, which is a representation of heaven, has heat and light as interrelated aspects. The more heat, the more light. The divine love and wisdom or heat and light are interrelated aspects. It is as though the unitary divine manifests in this primal duality. This mysterious and primal duality is everywhere present in Swedenborg. It is variously described as good-truth, charity-faith, wisdom-intelligence, will-understanding, essence-existence. The affective love or warmth is its heart, or innermost nature. The outer truth—faith, intelligence, understanding, existence—is the way it manifests itself. Man as a thing, a number, a mere existence is the shell, or outer manifestation, of this divine love. His inner life is divine love acting. When this inner love comes into act or charity the divine has manifested in existence and become real.

Swedenborg always gives this love a more fundamental role than truth, or the outer thingness of existence. This is so whether he is saying that feeling is more fundamental than thought or that charity is more important than faith. He was very firm that religions emphasizing faith were going toward the estranged, intellectual shell of existence. This love-feeling-charity is the will-like mustness of existence. Like the forces of nature, it must do, create, give birth to itself. Our needs with each other are just an aspect of this. The laws of nature are not textbook statements, they are the forces moving the thunderclouds. These are manifestations of the mustness of love. Swedenborg's concept is quite the opposite of an abstract idea. As the lightning flashes, thunder rolls, and the rain pours down on you—that is this mustness, must be, the willful heart of existence. If the idea doesn't seem concrete enough yet, stand there till the sky clears to sunshine! Go a step further. There is just one heart in all of existence. This Swedenborg called divine love. It is intimately joined inwardly with your own willfulness. I am very much in accord with Zen Buddhism's tendency not to be abstract about the concrete. In a Zen story a sincere student asks his master to show him the Buddha nature. The master says casually, "You just had breakfast. Did you wash your dishes?" This is a very precise answer to the student's question. The Buddha nature is to do the minor good that comes to your hand, i.e., wash the dishes. It would belie the Buddha nature to talk of goodness and leave someone else to wash the dishes. For me, Swedenborg has this same concreteness that is so well exemplified in Zen Buddhism, which is perhaps why the Zen master Daisetz Suzuki translated Swedenborg into Japanese.

Let us look at this primal duality in an opposite way. Insofar as I indentify with my outward aspects—myself as body, as so-and-so, as thought—I am denying or overlooking the root of my existence. I become a thing among things, in competition with other things for existence. We could also choose to enlarge our concept of identity to include the whole background of affects—feeling, love, life emerging. The truth is that both are real, inner and outer, love and truth, yin and yang,[35] and all the related dualities. This general duality is the source of the acts by which what wants to be becomes really something. In a human sense, it is the source of our need to understand what is and to be. The person who identifies both with the inner becoming and the outer body self is accepting their full scope and also the dependence of their existence. We do not make the background sea of feeling from which our inner lives emerge. We are the onlooking participants in the lives that emerge through us. The man whose identity is placed at the interface of feeling-love becomes real as this now experience, senses he is participating in a process larger than himself. He says to himself that there is more than himself. This is to acknowledge God (by whatever name). God here means that which is bigger than all of us. The one who searches within, into his own nature, searches for this Bigger One. The exploration of self, psychology, and the religions are fundamentally the same thing. The religious quest gives a comprehensive name to the larger One sought after. Psychology gives it more limited names (being, my nature, the integrated self, etc.) and waits to see its nature to know what it is.

If we turn this duality outward it is equally illuminating. Inward love, the life of the individual, flows into the body and act. Swedenborg was saying in a very real sense that the Lord suffers a stillbirth until man acts by the good that he knows. This primeval good is a kind of general impulse toward existence. It must become real, exist. What is the manifestation of the primal good? It is many and all existences. It is the whole physical universe. An existence for the primal good that is nearer to its real nature occurs when man feels, understands the good. Swedenborg speaks of this as the Second Coming of the Lord. The Lord comes here and there, willy-nilly, on the clouds of man's understanding. The Second Coming occurs when man understands the Word. Swedenborg used the Word to mean both the Bible and, inwardly, as God Himself. "Most persons believe that the Word or Divine Truth is nothing more than speech uttered by Jehovah, and a command that such a thing be done, but it is that very essential, from which, and through which, all things are" (AC 7678). The person whose understanding is opened and meets God knows the real Second Coming, the incarnation.

There is a more concrete form for this primal good to come into existence. In the concept of uses Swedenborg's whole tour of heaven and hell comes to earth in the commonplace. The good that is in us is nothing until it comes into existence as uses. The floor needs sweeping, something needs fixing, you are a shoemaker with shoes to repair, a friend needs you to hear him—uses. "Love is the end, wisdom the instrumental cause, and use is the effect; and use is the complex, containant, and base of wisdom and love; and use is such a complex and such a containant, that all things of love and all things of wisdom are actually in it; it is where they are all simultaneously present" (DLW 213). Use is where Divine Love comes to earth in actuality, in something done for the environment. Love-good yearns to be real. Just as wisdom is the form of good, our good acts are its becoming real. We are not the first cause of good, just as we are recipients of life, not its cause. The good man sees how much he is a participant, almost an onlooker, in the sequence of life processes. The evil man overly credits himself, evil meaning cutting off.

The heart of the difficulties in our life can be described in several ways. The Lord is the ultimately free. We are the image or representation of that freedom in our capacity to choose. The love that animates existence wills that we be free to choose. Because of the limitations of our existence we are partially bound and partially free. What we do with our corner of freedom sets our eternal existence. Heaven and hell are the polar opposites that illustrate the full scope of possibilities of this freedom. The general drift of the hierarchy of heaven is toward joining with others, loving, toward the unitary oneness of the Lord. The general drift of hell is toward separation, division, cutting off, and struggle against others. We clearly have the foretaste of both possibilities in this world.

In a sense our freedom is dreadful. Though we have sufficient road signs or guides, especially in the religious traditions, it is easy enough to doubt them and get lost with or without them. This freedom implies that it was meant that we should struggle, and each find his way on his own. Swedenborg was very clear that only what we accomplish with our own freedom lasts to eternity. We are not bound any other way. Also, the inner aspect of things belies outer appearance. He cites the case of madmen who, when their interiors were opened in the world of spirits, became quite sane. There are also men who look good in the light of this world but who become quite insane and bind themselves to hell when their interiors are opened. This is another sense in which our existences are contingent. Though we hope to be doing things right, we can't really judge until the outer shells of our existence are removed. And this is the judgment that the ancient tradition speaks of. In our corner of freedom we struggle in the dim light of our understanding and our habits. But it should be cheering to discover that we are judged by the inner quality or interior in our acts, not so much by the outer consequence.

Where do trials and tribulations fit into this? It was not meant that existence would be all smooth and simple, like being bottle-fed on divine pablum. Our existence must have the full range of possibilities. Darkness illuminates light. Can the infant who dies in innocence ascend to the highest heaven? Not immediately. The infant has much to learn. Trials and tribulation are echoed inwardly in the imagery of the inner life, which is one side of the guidance system; difficulties in the material world are the other side of it.

Swedenborg once remarked that if the Lord wished to condemn a man, he would give him all he wished. This would be the profoundest of all condemnations.

One of the difficulties between us and God is that we have our immediate needs in mind. The Lord rules existence in terms of our ultimate good. Our perspective is too small.

It has not been known that divine providence in all its procedure with man looks to his eternal state. It can look to nothing else because the Divine is infinite and eternal, and the infinite and eternal or the Divine is not in time; therefore all future things are present to it. It follows that there is eternity in all that the Divine does. But those who think from time and space perceive this with difficulty, not only because they love temporal things, but also because they think from what is on hand in the world and not from what is at hand in heaven; this is as remote to them as the ends of the earth. Those, however, who are in the Divine, inasmuch as they think from the Lord, think from what is eternal as well as from what is at present, asking themselves, "What is that which is not eternal?"

What a line: "What is that which is not eternal?"! It should be carved deeply over the door to one's study. But he continues:

"Is not the temporal relatively nothing and does it not become nothing when it is past?" The eternal is not so; it alone *is;* its *esse* has no end. To think thus is to think both from the present and the eternal, and when a man not only thinks so but lives so, the . . . divine providence looks in all its procedure to the state of his eternal life in heaven and guides to it. DP 59

The Lord, acting in relation to our ultimate good, can lead where we would not choose to go. A practical consequence of this is that the person having great troubles can look in them for usefulness. Swedenborg spoke of vastation, a kind of being brought down by the Lord. It happens here and even to angels in heaven. A depressed mood is a good example.

We go along feeling that all is going well only to be stopped and brought down by the depression. Depression destroys false values. It occurs when we presume too much, assume too much power or greatness for ourselves. God speaks,

> I form light and create darkness,
> > I make weal and create woe,
> > I am the Lord, who do all these things.

*   *   *

> "Woe to him who strives with his Maker,
> > an earthen vessel with the potter!
> Does the clay say to him who fashions it,
> > 'What are you making?'
> > or 'Your work has no handles?'
> Woe to him who says to a father,
> > 'What are you begetting?'
> > or to à woman, 'With what are you in travail?' "
> Thus says the Lord,
> > The Holy One of Israel, and his Maker:
> "Will you question me about my children,
> > or command me concerning the work of my hands?
> I make the earth,
> > and created man upon it;
> it was my hands that stretched out the heavens,
> > and I command all their host" (Isaiah 45:7–13).

We are the pot that should realize it was fashioned. The missing handles, the inconvenience of our existence, reflect in the trials and tribulations we question the most. These experiences would be rough and unfair except from the viewpoint of our eternal destiny. Our lives were not designed to be exactly as we wish.

The bringing down saves us in an eternal sense. This natural process can be cooperated with by looking for the usefulness in the bringing down of old values so that new ones may grow instead. Inwardly and outwardly we are educated in this schoolhouse world. The good person feels a respectful part of the more. The evil one cuts himself off by assuming he is the whole thing. Amplifying into other worlds, the cutting off is hell. Working with all the rest is heaven. This scope of existence illustrates our freedom and God's. Our limited freedom is the little image of God's. It is sinful to divide up the one life; love sees its unity.

There is a lovely undercurrent in Swedenborg, as in most religions that say there is only one life: "as you did it to one of the least of these my brethren, you did it to me" (Matthew 25:40). Out of this arises the Golden Rule, which is the heart of several religions besides Christianity. I participate in a life and so do you. Perhaps we are all the one life. . . . So the Eskimo who must kill a polar bear to live pauses to wish the bear's departing spirit well. The one who loves can see similarities, points of agreement, and possible union. The one who is cut off from himself cuts off others, and finds reasons for differences. In effect, the journey of this primal good from the Lord, through the heavens, through man into act is heading back to itself, the unity of all things that love intimates. The good I do for another unites us. All our goods or uses unite man into a heaven where we can sense the oneness of things, the Lord.

The following are section headings from *The Divine Providence:*

i   Heaven is conjunction with the Lord.
ii   By creation the human being is such that he can be conjoined more and more closely to the Lord.
iii The more one is conjoined to the Lord the wiser one becomes.
iv   The more closely one is conjoined to the Lord the happier one becomes.
v   The more closely one is conjoined to the Lord the more distinctly does he seem to himself to be his own, and the more plainly does he recognize that he is the Lord's. DP 27

Only theory suggests that to be the Lord's is to suffer a loss of freedom. The experience is one of being more in control, being able to exercise more power, and yet to know that the real power comes from beyond the little ego self. Freedom is to be able to do what one loves most. The Lord's man carries into act what he loves most. None of this is limited to high, noble-sounding acts. The man who loves laying bricks, and lays them well, for a fair price, is doing enough to realize heaven. A simple kindness to another person is the true precursor of heaven and has its immediate reward in the unity with the other person. Swedenborg always combined the highest and the lowest. In a real sense his exploration of heaven and hell leads to the opposite of otherworldliness. Heaven and hell are here all the time. Grasp the experience of making heaven and hell here to shape your eternal destiny as you choose. You already know heaven and hell, you already participate in a society of people like yourself in some spiritual realm; eventually you will see more fully how true this is.

Throughout, Swedenborg remained in touch with this world, with the simple and even with the material. He felt later that his long tour through science was really just preparation, where he learned how far his own projections and theorizing could carry him. He went too far with theory when he did his own anatomical dissections. Later he kept just to the anatomical observations of others. Swedenborg's capacity to remain grounded in the limited, simple, and obvious while also dealing with the highest truths of the spiritual worlds heightens his existential and mystical quality. Here, there; this, that; all others, myself; all one. The oneness of things is the always present, underlying reality. By referring to it as life, or even more personally as humanness, Swedenborg again remains in the here-now, real. Thank heavens God is human, and hence understandable. This is an underlying meaning of God appearing as Jesus Christ. Some like their God remote, others near at hand. What Swedenborg found and described was simultaneously both. The most ultimate of all is very near at hand. They are the same.

A critical question is: Who did Swedenborg say would be saved? Translating the ancient idea of being saved into the present context, those saved are experiencing the enlarging reality of existence. The damned suffer a constricted existence. They miss out. Swedenborg's answer to this question is more generous than that in most of the world's religious literature. All will be saved who act by the good that they know. I believe that this implies a struggle and search. Most people's highest good is not a simple cookbook set of rules. It is more of a struggle, like trying to understand and be helpful to a friend. What is really good for the friend is not always simple; it involves searching and trying to understand. The dictum that all will be saved who act by the good they know takes Swedenborg into the universal of religion. This church of all those who act by the good they know Swedenborg saw being established in heaven. It is the church of the New Jerusalem. One should always suspect that any term used in heaven has very broad, unitive meanings. The New Jerusalem is the New Church being established by the Lord, treated of in the Apocalypse (Chapters 21 and 22). It is to be the bride and wife of the Lamb. This is a lovely image of love, tenderness, and union between the initiating maleness of the Lord and the female receptivity of churches. It is human and yet sacred. The image carries with it all the associations of two lovers who want to be joined and even of the troubles and misunderstandings that arise between lovers. In his *Brief Exposition of the Doctrine of the New Church* (99–104), Swedenborg showed the many biblical passages in which Jerusalem was obviously not simply a city, or even a church in the limited sense. "Behold I create a *new heaven and a new earth,* and the former shall not be remembered; behold *I will create Jerusalem,* an exhultation, and her people a gladness, that I may exult over *Jerusalem,* and be glad over my people" Isaiah 65:17–19. He went on to cite many passages with a similar import (Isaiah 62:1–4, 11, 12; Isaiah 52: 1, 2, 6, 9; Zephaniah 3: 14–17, 20; Zechariah 8:3, 20–23; Joel 4:17–21, and others).

The mystery becomes clear when we consider who is to be saved? Who is to find salvation?

[I]t is plain that the church of the Lord is not here, nor there, but that it is everywhere, both within those kingdoms where the church is, and outside them, where men live according to the precepts of charity. Hence it is that the church of the Lord is scattered through the whole world, and yet it is one; for when life makes the church, and not doctrine separate from life, then the church is one, but when doctrine makes the church, then there are many. AC 8152

He is very clear: the church is within and without the Christian church. It is everywhere that men act in charity to each other. It is the differences in doctrine that seem to separate churches. When you look at their life, then it is one. He refers to the great variety of societies in heaven and yet they act as a one, the Grand Man. "Varieties in matters of doctrine and of worship are like the varieties of the senses and of the viscera in man" (AC 1285). And like man, they form one being.

The church of the Lord consists of all those, whosoever they are, who are in truths derived from good. AE 20 The church of the Lord is spread over the whole globe, and thus is universal; and all those are in it who have lived in the good of charity according to their religious belief. HH 328

Many other passages could also be cited (DP 325, HH 318 f.). In a beautiful passage Swedenborg interpreted the line from Exodus 20:24, "In every place I shall put the memorial of My name." The memorial of My name is placed when a man acts charitably toward others. This is the name-nature of the One being commemorated. In another passage Swedenborg again affirmed the necessity and beauty of great differences and variety.

It is similar with the spiritual things of the Church, the opposites of which are related to evil and falsity. These opposites, however, are not from the Lord but from man, who is endowed with free will, and this he can turn to a good or to an evil use. So also is it the case with darkness and cold; these do not come from the sun, but from the earth, which by its revolutions successively withdraws and turns away. Yet without this turning and withdrawal there would be neither day nor year, and consequently neither inanimate nor animate created things upon it. TCR 736

Then, to emphasize this acceptance of variety in religious matters, Swedenborg casually referred to something he heard angels say in heaven! "I have heard that churches which are in a variety of goods and truths are like so many jewels in a king's crown" (TCR 763).

It is so clear that Swedenborg was speaking of the heart of religion that transcends the boundaries of creeds, nations, cultures, times, people. All who act in the good that they know will be saved. I believe this acting is not a simple matter of following a set of rules. The good we know is larger than ourselves. It involves a searching, trying. Good is of the life, life trying to find and act on its highest capacities, life discovering itself.

Swedenborg had more followers in the 1800s than he has now. Some of these followers felt they should act to give this Church of the New Jerusalem a home, an institution in which it could be ultimated and realized here on earth. (In part this resulted from the rejection of Swedenborg by the established churches.) This became a small Protestant sect that, in time, proceeded to split into liberal and conservative factions. Now the several branches of the churches of the New Jerusalem range from those who see Swedenborg as simply a gifted man to those who see his word almost as sacred as the word of God. Often these groups refer to themselves as Swedenborgian. Swedenborg clearly would have been opposed to attaching his name to any church. In relation to churches he was just another servant of the Lord. His name didn't matter.

I respectfully differ with the followers of Swedenborg who established churches of the New Jerusalem. Though it is perfectly appropriate for people of like mind to join together under any name, I believe that in this instance many of them tended to miss the great universality of what Swedenborg was pointing to. Often Swedenborgians wonder why their most favored, greatest of all dispensations resulted in several poor tiny churches. Perhaps they are being tested? Perhaps its day to sweep over the whole earth is yet to come?

I belong to the group of scholars that feels that the Church of the New Jerusalem is well established, the largest church of all, the community of all those of different cultures, languages, creeds, and styles of living who act by the good they know. I am in accord with the noted theologian Walter Marshall Horton that Swedenborg's followers' claim to an exclusive esoteric revelation unnecessarily cut him off from the fellowship of other churches.[36] His is not an exclusive revelation. Though it is unique in some ways, he is talking about the heart of all religions. Others also have illuminated the heart of religions. The Church of the New Jerusalem is founded. It is the communion and fellowship of all those who act from the good that they know. In fact, Horton calls Swedenborg one of the greatest and earliest ecumenicists in an age that had not yet heard the term. The real Church of the New Jerusalem could find Swedenborg illuminating any religious tradition, including primitive ones. It is important to understand this. By focusing on man, the essentials of the human, Swedenborg was transcending any particular culture or time. Though he was very much a western man who thought in terms of the Christian tradition, he broke through to the universal. Hence people like Daisetz Suzuki (a Zen Buddhist) and Gopaul Chetty[37] (a Hindu) could become followers of Swedenborg and yet remain in their own faiths.

It is difficult for some to understand truly the universality of what Swedenborg points to. They feel safest and most comfortable in a set of specific doctrines and ceremonies. This is right for them. But they easily lapse from this to the implication that "their way is the one right way." Look at the great diversity of faces, ages, skin colors, clothes, styles of living. Thus, while we like to latch onto the "one right way," nature herself is diverse. If nothing else we need many churches, many doctrines, many traditions to accommodate the diversity of man. In dealing with the essentials of good, of the life of man, Swedenborg looked beyond the masks of diversity to the One Life. There is no problem in the distinct and great diversities of societies in heaven coordinating as the one life of the Grand Man, the image of the Very Human Lord. Diversity-Oneness. As the Zen koan goes, "What is it, that, forever changing, remains exactly the same?" Forever changing, the many churches, doctrines; remain the same, the One Life they speak of.

Others have asked whether Swedenborg would support the idea of reincarnation, which is prominent in some eastern religions. The idea itself is often misunderstood. In the Hindu tradition it isn't the personal, little me that is reincarnated. It is the general tendencies or the primal monad, of which I am the current edition, that reincarnates. Or another way of saying it is that it is something closer to the Divine than to me that reincarnates. Well, of course, the Lord reincarnates through the whole of existence, since He is the One Life that is the source of all lives. I believe the personal experience of reincarnation is a step on the way to the larger identity. The social usefulness of the idea lies in the implication that I could be this or that kind of life, which again is a step on the way to seeing the One Life. It is in the direction of love, empathy, understanding, respect for others. Yet, regarding the personal identity, Swedenborg clearly stressed the uniqueness of each one. I am these basic tendencies and qualities, and I will be through the whole of creation. So I'd be inclined to say that outwardly Swedenborg did not support reincarnation, but as inwardly understood, he did. Both are true. Outwardly I am this unique person, but my real nature drifts toward the One Life that reincarnates through the whole of time. The advantage of the stress on the uniqueness of the person is that it says, here, in the very qualities that I am, is the Divine. It stresses the obligation to find the way through the immediate consciousness of being. But, as indicated above, there is also truth and usefulness in the idea of reincarnation. I would not wish to denigrate another doctrine that contains real truth and usefulness.

After so much praise and support of Swedenborg I would like to ask if he was ever clearly wrong in his spiritual works. The answer is probably an unclear yes. His most misleading work is *Earths in the Universe,* in which he presented the reports of spirits who claimed to be humans from planets in our solar system, including our own moon. These are probably what Swedenborg calls "enthusiastic" spirits. They report in a convincing manner whatever one wants to hear. Swedenborg must have heard that there was at least little atmosphere on the moon, so these moon spirits have an odd way of speaking that conserves air. He could not have known what is now known of our moon. For there to be humanlike life on our moon is at least extremely unlikely, if not impossible. Swedenborg appeared to believe the reports of spirits from our moon, Mercury, Mars, Jupiter, and the other planets. Because he could not have known better, he appeared to have been taken in by some enthusiastic spirits. As one Swedenborgian exclaimed, thank heavens he was at least wrong in one thing. His whole system is not to be taken on his authority. He derived it from experience. We are to check it by our own lives. This flaw in his reporting reminds us that we are each on our own, to find our own way.

But when we look closer at the odd matter of moon spirits there is a strange note of the real in the midst of it. When Swedenborg relates the moon spirits to the zyphoid cartilage in the Grand Man, we suddenly realize our guide is referring to something subjective that we don't really understand (*Earths in the Universe*, 111). The rib signifies the proprium, or ego (AC 138, 147). The real spirit of these moon spirits is the coming together or forefront of egotism. If these spirits are really some kind of spiritual tomfoolery, it is curious that they relate to the area of the Grand Man that reflects egotism, from which we might expect pretentious reporting. Even when misled, he was reporting from some subjective realm that has its own strange truths.

In a similar way I would reserve judgment when Swedenborg reported a low status for certain groups in the spiritual world (i.e., Mohammedans, certain Roman Catholics, papists, the Dutch people, etc.). It would be very difficult, for instance, to be a Mohammedan and appreciate Swedenborg. Repeatedly the Mohammedans appear in low status until they drift in an essentially Christian direction in the spiritual worlds. This same kind of negative note appears in relation to several other groups. In any event I think this a diplomatic error because it makes it difficult for whole groups to appreciate Swedenborg. If one assembled all his references to Mohammedans, for instance, a more subtle picture would emerge in which he was talking about a type of spiritual error, but the error does not apply to all members of the group. There is always the saving grace of those who act charitably out of the good they know, regardless of the group they are from. For those who are members of a group that Swedenborg found in low spiritual status, I would say that even in looking at his work it would be well if we could be charitable, reserve judgment, and be guided by the good we see reflected.

It is often asked whether others can go the same route and follow Swedenborg. The answer is not simple.

> Upon being asked several times why no one besides himself enjoyed such revelations and intercourse with spirits, he answered that every person might enjoy it now as in the times of the Old Testament, but the real hindrance is that men at the present time are so carnally minded. Docs II, p. 559

Looking back, Swedenborg saw that his whole life was designed for this work. The hard facts of rocks, engineering, astronomy, and anatomy were his training ground. He was trained to observe and report factually. This he did through all the worlds. His style was relatively dry and academic except in certain of his religious works where his words burn with life. And of course no one opens up the life of God except as God permits. The personal quality of Swedenborg's whole life was a real key to what was given to him to see and experience. Also, in reviewing the path he came over, Swedenborg reported it as quite dangerous. Unleashing the inner springs of mind is no minor matter. The main purport of Swedenborg's work is that others could do as much and some would do more, but it was a journey he didn't recommend to anyone. Madness could lie that way, depending upon the quality of the life.

It is very clear that Swedenborg would recommend to other seekers that they live by the good they know and seek in the revealed Word for anything they want. He found so much in the Word that this is no minor recommendation. He would also hope some would find use in his writings. Most of his later life was spent in just making his findings available cheaply to others. For this reason I do not belong to any church called Swedenborgian, but I do support the work of the Swedenborgian publishing societies. Those who put Swedenborg's own works on a pedestal should know that it wasn't his own tendency. He was a servant helping the understanding of the great work, the Word of God. If I could now ask Swedenborg one question it would be this: Are there other authoritative Words of God than the Christian Bible? Just as the New Jerusalem is everywhere, I believe the Word of God is also, for after all, it is our very lives, which are here, handy, to be read. This is the Word of God written on the heart.

Clearly Swedenborg would encourage the search. Act by the good that you know. Ask and more will be given. And insofar as the search is full-bodied, strong, and persistent it is a good given by the Lord. For it is the Lord who searches through the clouds of our misunderstandings. The Second Coming is eminently possible. And having come the feeling is, oh yes, of course, how could it be forgotten?

All the other worlds are present in the root nature of humanness. In this full sense we participate in and issue forth from all there is. We are the presence of all the worlds. And all the worlds, and worlds of worlds, are aspects of the One. And this One is always present as life itself, the Very Human.

Key to Abbreviations
of Works Cited

Quotations from Swedenborg are referenced to indicate the title and numbers (paragraph). For instance, AC 2101 is the *Arcana Coelestia,* paragraph 2101. Almost all of his works have conveniently numbered paragraphs. Where this is not so, a page number is indicated. There will be some little difference in wording if the reader finds a different translation than the one used here. I used a variety of translations from the U.S. Swedenborg Foundation and the London Swedenborg Society.

AC	*Arcana Coelestia,* 3 vols.
AE	*Apocalypse Explained,* 6 vols.
DF	*Doctrine of Faith* (in *Four Doctrines of the New Jerusalem*)
DL	*Doctrine of Life* (in *Four Doctrines of the New Jerusalem*)
DLDW	*Divine Love and the Divine Wisdom;* also called *The Doctrine of Uses,* excerpted from the *Apocalypse Explained*
DLW	*Divine Love and Wisdom*
Docs	R. L. Tafel, *Documents Concerning Swedenborg,* 3 vols.

DP	*Divine Providence*
DS	*Doctrine of Sacred Scripture* (in *Four Doctrines of the New Jerusalem*)
HD	*Heavenly Doctrine*
HH	*Heaven and Hell*
JD	*Journal of Dreams*
ML	*Marital Love,* also called *Conjugial Love*
RP	*Rational Psychology*
SD	*Spiritual Diary,* 5 vols.
TCR	*True Christian Religion*
WE	*Word Explained*
WH	*White Horse,* excerpted from the *Arcana Coelestia*

Guide to Swedenborg's Writings

In case the reader wishes to explore Swedenborg further, the following is provided as an guide. There are various translations of these writings. In general, the more recent the translation, the easier it is to read.

Most Widely Read

A few of Swedenborg's works have a lyrical quality that has made them universally popular. They also carry the essence of his discoveries in the clearest and most beautiful form. *Heaven and Hell* gives a relatively complete description of those worlds, yet the reader will see much of the structure of mind and existence implied in it. *Divine Love and Wisdom* goes from the heart of existence to man's situation. The feeling-love side of Swedenborg is clearest here. *Divine Providence* gives the design of existence with special reference to man's life.

The Spiritual Worlds

Heaven and Hell is the his basic description. There are important clues scattered throughout the *Arcana Coelestia* and especially in sections between chapters. The *Spiritual Diary* contains an unorganized array of experiences in spiritual worlds. Odhner's *The Spiritual World*[38] and *Spirits and Men*[39] are very competent scholarly works bringing together everything relevant from Swedenborg.

The Human Mind

Swedenborg doesn't distinguish between the spiritual and the psychological so all his theological works bear on this area. His three most popular works cited above are relevant here. Add to them *The Divine Love and The Divine Wisdom,* especially on the doctrine of uses. See also *Heavenly Doctrine,* especially on the internal and external of man. The little work *Intercourse of Soul and Body* is also useful. Odhner has a scholarly survey, *The Human Mind.*[40] The *Arcana Coelestia* is very rich on the nuances of inner states, too rich for all but the specialist. Often people refer to Swedenborg's early psychology, such as *Rational Psychology,* as his principal work in this area. It was so limited in conception compared to the works following his enlightenment that it is of little use. See also his *Journal of Dreams* to find this psychoanalyst at work on his dreams.

Biography and Introduction to His Works

Often a tracing of his history is linked with a survey of his basic teachings. G. Trobridge, *Swedenborg Life and Teach-*

ing, is a popular and competent work in this area.[41] For a fine survey see John Spalding, *Introduction to Swedenborg's Religious Thought.*[42] Another work that combines both history and teachings is Sigstedt, *The Swedenborg Epic.*[43] These three volumes really grasp Swedenborg. A strangely unsympathetic work that especially tries to see him as a spiritualist is Toksvig, *Emanuel Swedenborg.*[44] Though Swedenborg had much to do with spirits, he didn't recommend that anyone else follow him in this. The issue for him was the nature of existence, not communion with the dead. Jonsson, *Emanuel Swedenborg,* is only competent on him as a scientist.[45] Acton, *Introduction to the Word Explained,* is one of the best books available on Swedenborg's spiritual development.[46] There are a number of works which handily gather together critical quotations that illuminate his position on a number of points. See Synnestvedt, *The Essential Swedenborg;*[47] Warren, *A Compendium of the Theological Writings of E. Swedenborg,* the longest of these;[48] Smyth and Wunsch, *The Gist of Swedenborg;*[49] Spalding, *Golden Thoughts;*[50] Ager, *The Path of Life,* now out of print.[51]

Correspondences

The idea of correspondences is fairly well scattered through all his theological works. See especially *Divine Providence, The Divine Love and The Divine Wisdom,* and sections in Volumes IV–VI of *The Arcana Coelestia.* For specific correspondences see *The Dictionary of Bible Imagery,*[52] *The Dictionary of Correspondences,*[53] and *The Swedenborg Concordance.*[54] Worcester, *The Language of Parable,* makes the whole matter clear and creditable.[55] A similar but older work is Brayley, *Natural Phenomena and Their Spiritual Lessons.*[56] Odhner, *The Divine Allegory,* shows correspondences with the geography of the Holy Land, a matter that plays a large role in the Bible.[57] See also Worcester, *Physiological Correspondences,* now out of print.[58]

Biblical Interpretation

Swedenborg's masterwork in this area is clearly the twelve-volume *Arcana Coelestia,* which treats principally of Genesis and Exodus but shows parallels from almost every other part of the Bible. See also his six-volume *Apocalypse Explained* and the shorter two-volume *Apocalyse Revealed,* which is available in a commendable modern one-volume translation by Alice Sechrist. His *Prophets and Psalms* is almost too brief an interpretation. To trace Swedenborg's comments on any passage of the Bible, see Searle, *General Index to Swedenborg's Scripture Quotations.*[59] A beautiful analysis of the complexities of the *Arcana* is Wunsch, *The World Within the Bible.*[60] Followers of Swedenborg have developed masterful studies of different books of the Bible. I'll mention just a few: Maclagan, *The Book of Deuteronomy;*[61] Odhner, *Saul, David and Solomon;*[62] Mitchell, *Parables of the Old Testament;*[63] Bruce, *Commentary on Matthew;*[64] Fischer, *Commentary on The Book of Ezekial,*[65] and others.

Reference Works

By far the largest and most monumental guide to Swedenborg is Potts's six-volume *Swedenborg Concordance.*[66] When one reads how Potts pulled together and translated these passages it seems he deserves a special commendation in heaven. With the *Concordance* one can trace Swedenborg's most important comments on any subject. This work is not complete, but it is quite impressive and useful anyway. To trace what Swedenborg says on any biblical passage, see

Searle, *General Index to Swedenborg's Scripture Quotations.*[67] For correspondences, see the *Dictionary of Bible Imagery.*[68] For definitions of all Swedenborg's key ideas, see Bogg, *A Glossary of the Meaning of Specific Terms and Phrases Used by Swedenborg.*[69] A glossary sounds like a dull academic work, this is not. For a mind-shattering experience I recommend reading it to see the sweep of Swedenborg's ideas. In the back of volume 2 of *Posthumous Theological Works* is a complete bibliography of Swedenborg's 237 works. The hundreds of commentaries on Swedenborg range from the almost childish to the very gifted. The *New Church Reader's Guide* helps a good deal with their classification.[70]

Publishers

All of his psychological/theological works and many of his scientific works and commentaries on him are available from these publishers. They may also be consulted on any matter pertaining to Swedenborg's works.

The Swedenborg Foundation, 139 East 23rd St., New York, N.Y. 10010

The Swedenborg Society, 20 Bloomsbury Way, London, W.C. 1A, England.

Swedenborg Verlag, Appollostrasse 2, 8032 Zurich, Switzerland.

Swedenborg Publisher, 136 Onuma-cho, Kodaira-shi, Tokyo, Japan.

REFERENCES

1. Borge, Jorge Luis, *Selected Poems 1923–1927,* trans. Richard Howard and Cesar Rennert (New York: Delacorte, 1972). Permission granted.

2. Emerson, Ralph W., *Representative Men* (Boston: Houghton Mifflin, 1930), pp. 102–103.

3. Mirt, J. A., "Medical Pathfinders on Postage Stamps," *Journal of the American Medical Association* 206 (1908):No. 4.

4. Tafel, R. L., *Documents Concerning Swedenborg* (London: Swedenborg Society, 1875), 1:392.

5. Swedenborg, Emanuel, *A Philosopher's Note Book* (Ann Arbor, Mich.: University Microfilms, 1970).

   ———, *Psychologica* (Philadelphia: Swedenborg Scientific Association, 1923).

   ———, *Psychological Transactions* (Philadelphia: Swedenborg Scientific Association, 1955).

   ———, *Rational Psychology* (Philadelphia: Swedenborg Scientific Association, 1950).

6. Swedenborg, *Journal of Dreams* (Bryn Athyn, Pa.: Academy Book Room, 1918).

   ———, *The Spiritual Diary,* 5 vols. Vol. 1 (London: The Swedenborg Society, 1962); Vols. 2–5, (Bryn Athyn, Pa.: Academy Book Room, 1962).

7. Swedenborg, *Spiritual Diary* (London: James Speirs, 1883), no. 3464.

8. Van Dusen, Wilson, *The Natural Depth in Man* (New York: Harper & Row, 1972).

9. Sartre, Jean-Paul, *The Psychology of Imagination.* (New York: Citadel Press, 1961).

10. Silberer, Herbert. *Report on a Method of Eliciting and Observing Certain Symbolic Hallucination Phenomena in David Rapaport: Organization and Pathology of Thought* (New York: Columbia University Press, 1951).

11. Mann, Kristine, "The Self-Analysis of Emanuel Swedenborg," *The Review of Religion* (1946): 266–293. This is a study by a Jungian analyst. Mann assumed that Jung's Self could not be the God within, hence Swedenborg didn't reach the Self. I see Swedenborg's ~~God~~ and the Self as the same, hence he did integrate.

12. Ehrenwald, Jan, *New Dimensions of Deep Analysis* (New York: Allen and Unwin, 1954).

13. Behanan, K. T., *Yoga* (New York: Macmillan, 1937); Bernard, Thomas, *Hatha Yoga* (New York: Columbia University Press, 1945).

14. Mann, "Self-Analysis of Swedenborg."

15. Acton, Alfred, *An Introduction to the Word Explained.* (Bryn Athyn, Pa.: Academy of the New Church, 1927), p. 115.

16. Barnitz, Harry W., *Existentialism and the New Christianity* (New York: Philosophical Library, 1969).

17. Anderson, H. H. and Anderson, Gladys, eds., *An Introduction to Projective Techniques.* (Englewood Cliffs, N.J.: Prentice-Hall, 1951).

18. Van Dusen, *Natural Depth in Man.*

19. Ibid.

20. Iungerich, Eldred E., *The Soul and Its Representations* (Edinburgh: Turnbull and Spears, 1936).

21. Lao-Tzu, *Tao Te Ching* (London: John Murry, 1950). There are many translations of this little, quite profound, Chinese work.

22. Van Dusen, *Natural Depth in Man.*

23. Healy, William; Bronner, Augusta; and Bowers, Anna, *The Structure and Meaning of Psychoanalysis* (New York: Knopf, 1931).

24. Marx, Melvin, and Hillix, William. *Systems and Theories in Psychology* (New York: McGraw-Hill, 1963).

25. All the incidents cited in this chapter are described in greater detail in R. L. Tafel, *Documents Concerning the Life and Character of Emanuel Swedenborg,* 3 vols. (London: Swedenborg Society, 1890). These volumes are now scarce. They cite every known source for the incidents and even make detailed comparisons where several accounts variously describe one incident. I've omitted the tedious scholarship and taken the most likely account where observers dif-

fered. References to the documents are given in the form Docs II, p. 621.

26. Jung, Carl, *The Collected Works of C. G. Jung* (Princeton: Princeton University Press, 1953), vol. 12.

27. Harrower, Molly, *Appraising Personality: An Introduction to the Projective Techniques* (New York: F. Watts, 1964).

28. Dunbar, Flanders, *Emotions and Bodily Changes* (New York: Columbia University Press, 1947).

29. Worcester, John, *Physiological Correspondences* (Boston: New Church Union, 1889).

30. Fisher, C., and Dement, W. C., "Studies on the Psychopathology of Sleep and Dreams," *American Journal of Psychiatry*, 119 (1963): 1160–1168.

31. Van Dusen, *Natural Depth in Man*.

32. Horton, Walter Marshall, *Emanuel Swedenborg, His Significance for Contemporary Theology* (New York: Swedenborg Foundation, 1965).

33. Alexander, George M., *The Handbook of Biblical Personalities* (Greenwich, Conn.: Seabury Press, 1962).

34. Iungerich, *The Soul and Its Representations*.

35. Lao-Tzu, *Tao Te Ching*.

36. Horton, *Emanuel Swedenborg: His Vision of a United Christianity* (New York: Swedenborg Foundation, 1965).

37. Chetty, D. Gopaul, *New Light upon Indian Philosophy or Swedenborg and Saiva Siddhanta* (London: J. M. Dent, 1923).

Guide to Swedenborg's Writings

38. Odhner, Hugo, *The Spiritual World* (Bryn Athyn, Pa.: Academy Publishing Committee, 1968).

39. Odhner, *Spirits and Man* (Bryn Athyn, Pa.: Academy Book Room, 1960).

40. Odhner, *The Human Mind, Its Faculties and Degrees* (Bryn Athyn, Pa.: Swedenborg Scientific Association, 1969).

41. Trobridge, George, *Swedenborg, Life and Teaching* (London: Swedenborg Society, 1945).

42. Spalding, John, *Introduction to Swedenborg's Religious Thought* (New York: Swedenborg Publishing Association, 1956).

43. Sigstedt, Cyriel, *The Swedenborg Epic* (New York: Bookman Associates, 1952).

44. Toksvig, Signe, *Emanuel Swedenborg, Scientist and Mystic,* (New Haven: Yale University Press, 1948).

45. Jonsson, Inge, *Emanuel Swedenborg* (New York: Twayne, 1971).

46. Acton, Alfred, *An Introduction to* The Word Explained (Bryn Athyn, Pa.: Academy of the New Church, 1927).

47. Synnestvedt, Sig, *The Essential Swedenborg* (New York: The Swedenborg Foundation, 1970).

48. Warren, Samuel, *A Compendium of the Theological Writings of Emanuel Swedenborg* (London: Swedenborg Society, 1954).

49. Smyth, Julian, and Wunsch, William, *The Gist of Swedenborg* (New York: Swedenborg Foundation, 1920).

50. Spalding, *Golden Thoughts* (London: Swedenborg Society, 1953).

51. Ager, John, *The Path of Life* (New York: New Church Press, 1913).

52. Sechrist, Alice, *The Dictionary of Bible Imagery* (New York: Swedenborg Foundation, 1973).

53. Bolles, Charles, *Dictionary of Correspondences or Representatives* (New York: Swedenborg Foundation, 1955).

54. Potts, John, *The Swedenborg Concordance* (London: Swedenborg Society, 1957 6 vols.).

55. Worcester, William, *The Language of Parable* (New York: New Church Press, date unknown).

56. Brayley, Ann, *Natural Phenomena and Their Spiritual Lessons* (London: Speirs, 1870).

57. Odhner, *The Divine Allegory* (New York: Swedenborg Foundation, 1954).

58. Worcester, John, *Physiological Correspondences* (Boston: New Church Union, 1889).

59. Searle, Arthur, *General Index to Swedenborg's Scripture Quotations* (London: Swedenborg Society, 1954).

60. Wunsch, William, *The World Within the Bible* (New York: New Church Press, 1929).

61. Maclagan, Henry, *The Book of Deuteronomy* (London: New Church Press, 1914).

62. Odhner, *Saul, David and Solomon* (Bryn Athyn, Pa.: General Church Publication Committee, 1967).

63. Mitchell, Edward, *The Parables of the Old Testament Explained* (Philadelphia: Wm. Alden, 1903).

64. Bruce, William, *Commentary on St. Matthew* (London: Pitman, 1867).

65. Fischer, Robert, *Commentary on Ezekiel* (Boston: Mass. New Church Union, 1925).

66. See n. 54 above.
67. See n. 59 above.
68. See n. 52 above.
69. Bogg, John, *A Glossary of Specific Terms and Phrases Used by Swedenborg* (London: Swedenborg Society, 1915).
70. General Church Publication Committee, *New Church Reader's Guide* (Bryn Athyn, Pa.: General Church Publication Committee, date unknown).

74 75 76 77 10 9 8 7 6 5 4 3 2 1